MANY TABLES
The Eucharist in the New Testament
and Liturgy Today

DENNIS E. SMITH
HAL E. TAUSSIG

MANY TABLES

*The Eucharist
in the New Testament
and Liturgy Today*

SCM PRESS
London

TRINITY PRESS INTERNATIONAL
Philadelphia

First published 1990

SCM Press Ltd
26–30 Tottenham Road
London N1 4BZ

Trinity Press International
3725 Chestnut Street
Philadelphia, Pa, 19104

British Library Cataloguing in Publication Data

Smith, Dennis E.
Many tables: the Eucharist in the New Testament and
liturgy today.
I. Title II. Taussig
264.36

ISBN 0–334–02443–9

Library of Congress Cataloging-in-Publication Data

Smith, Dennis Edwin, *1941–*
Many tables: the Eucharist in the New Testament
and liturgy today
/ Dennis E. Smith and Hal Taussig.
    p.   cm.
Includes bibliographical references.
ISBN 0–334–02443–9
    1. Lord's Supper—History. 2. Lord's Supper
(Liturgy). I. Taussig, Hal II. Title.
BV823.S63   1990
264'.36'09—dc20   90–31941

Photoset by J&L Composition Ltd, Filey, North Yorkshire
and printed in Great Britain by
Billing & Sons Ltd, Worcester

For
Ray Henry, dervish,
and
Barbara McBride-Smith,
life partner

Contents

Acknowledgments

This project grew out of our separate histories and interests. We met at the national meetings of the Jesus Seminar, sponsored by the Westar Institute, and discovered a remarkable convergence of interests and passions. We experienced further growth in collaboration thereafter, especially in an intensive week in monkish devotion to writing, review, debate, and revision, in Philadelphia in the summer of 1989.

Special thanks is due to Robert Funk, whose gift of bringing together scholars once again proved magical, especially as it applied to our collaboration. We are deeply grateful to Burton Mack, who has served as mentor and adopted mentor, and has given scholarly and personal inspiration to us in this work. Finally we need to thank the many others of our friends and colleagues in the circles of scholarship and church who have nurtured us in our separate and collaborative quests.

Barbara McBride-Smith's creativity in the performing arts has been an inspiration to the writing of this book.

Many people have helped us understand the importance of the celebrative and the liturgical. Absolutely central to this process has been the wisdom of John Quick, Susan Cole Cady, Heath Allen, and – once again – Burton Mack. Two institutions have been willing and winsome laboratories for this process in important ways: Calvary United Methodist Church in Philadelphia, at which many of the eucharistic liturgies were used, and Sophia's House, a spirituality center in Philadelphia. Others without whose creativity and support we would have foundered are Arthur Brandenburg, Marian Ronan, Roy Reed, Lynne McMahon, and Anne DeViron. Special thanks for insight relative to the "Eucharistic Celebration of Black History" is due to Nora Lewis and Ruth Meachem.

Permission for "You Send Your Breath" and "I Hear You Knocking" granted by Heath Allen; for "A Eucharistic Prayer Based on Matthew 11" by Harper and Row, Publishers; and for "Church Going" by Marvell Press.

All biblical quotations are from the Revised Standard Version. Quotations from the Mishnah are taken from Jacob Neusner, ed., *The Mishnah* (New Haven: Yale University Press 1988). Quotations from other ancient documents are taken from the Loeb Classical Library edition where available; otherwise the source for the translation is given in the notes.

Our process has been the following. Dennis Smith proposed the collaborative venture. Over the next eighteen months we proceeded together to conceptualize, outline, and frame the entire project. Smith's work on ancient meals, Taussig's efforts in ritual theory and liturgical practice, and both our training as New Testament scholars formed the basis for the exciting new thesis that emerged. Smith then drafted chapters 1–3 and Taussig chapters 4–6 before collaborative revisions were made.

· 1 ·

Worship at a Crossroad

Once I am sure there's nothing going on
I step inside, letting the door thud shut.
Another church: matting, seats, and stone,
And little books; sprawlings of flowers, cut
For Sunday, brownish now; some brass and stuff
Up at the holy end; the small neat organ;
And a tense, musty, unignorable silence,
Brewed God knows how long. Hatless, I take off
My cycle-clips in awkward reverence. . .

I sign the book, donate an Irish sixpence,
Reflect the place was not worth stopping for.

Yet stop I did: in fact I often do,
And always end much at a loss like this,
Wondering what to look for; wondering, too,
When churches fall completely out of use
What we shall turn them into, if we shall keep
A few cathedrals chronically on show,
Their parchment, place and pyx in locked cases,
And let the rest rent-free to rain and sheep.
Shall we avoid them as unlucky places?

. . . I wonder who
Will be the last, the very last, to seek
This place for what it was; one of the crew
That tap and jot and know what rood-lofts were?
Some ruin-bibber, randy for antique,

Or Christmas-addict, counting on a whiff
Of gown-and-bands and organ-pipes and myrrh?

. . . A serious house on serious earth it is,
In whose blent air all our compulsions meet,
Are recognized, and robed as destinies.
And that much never can be obsolete,
Since someone will forever be surprising
A hunger in himself to be more serious,
And gravitating with it to this ground,
Which, he once heard, was proper to grow wise in,
If only that so many dead lie round.

(From "Church Going," by Philip Larkin[1])

To paraphrase Larkin, is there anything going on in the
churches? Are churches today to be seen as museums that
preserve relics from the past? Are they obsolete in the
contemporary world? Larkin's is a pessimistic view. Yet in
the end he is oddly nostalgic. He longs for that which the
church used to be, that which for him would fulfill a "hunger
in himself to be more serious."

It has been said that this poem is "as important a statement
of the mid-twentieth century consciousness as Arnold's
'Dover Beach' was of the mid-nineteenth."[2] Though it was
written in 1954, it has a ring of authenticity to it even today.
It speaks of the gulf that exists between contemporary, jaded
humankind, for whom nonbelief appears to be the only
option, and the archaic, even dead, language spoken by the
church. Yet there is a hunger there, a hunger the church used
to fill. Can it do so again?

What happens inside the church doors is its liturgy. It is
there that life and fulfillment should be found, but too often
today liturgy seems stale and lacking in vitality. The problem
is not a lack of faith so much as it is a lack of life in the liturgy
itself. In our liturgies we have let our emphasis on preserving
traditional forms and expressions overrule attempts to give
vital expression to the life and faith of contemporary
participants.

This is especially true with that part of the liturgy that is known as the Lord's Supper or eucharist. Though the practice of this sacrament is still central to the piety of most Christians today, here especially there is often a lifelessness and lack of connection with life as it is now lived. This need not be, however. The tradition is alive with meaning that we have too often overlooked. And liturgy can more effectively address the contemporary situation if we can learn better how to apply it to the aesthetic and symbolic language of today's culture.

These perspectives are not entirely new. Indeed, liturgical renewal in various forms has been underway for several generations now. It is important, then, to trace some of the recent developments in this endeavor in order to understand how far we have come and what issues have emerged.

Recent attempts at liturgical renewal

Various attempts at liturgical renewal have been made in the recent past. Most representative, and perhaps most important, have been the discussions that have taken place under the auspices of the World Council of Churches.

For several years "ecumenical convergence" has been sought in the sacraments of baptism and eucharist. Significant progress has been made in recent years, resulting in Faith and Order Paper No. 111 on *Baptism, Eucharist and Ministry*, published by the World Council of Churches in 1982.[3] This statement was developed at the Faith and Order Conference in Lima in 1982, but represents the culmination of a "fifty-year process of study."[4] The paper has attempted to define common elements in these sacraments among the various churches. By producing such a document it is hoped that the churches may be brought closer together toward inter-communion or mutual recognition of the various liturgical traditions.

To be sure, the issue to which these discussions have been directed is that of divisiveness in the Christian community. That is to say, liturgical renewal has been defined primarily in terms of ecumenical concerns. Revitalization *per se* has not been the primary focus. Rather, the approach has been to seek for common grounds of faith and practice.

Nevertheless, these dialogues by leaders and scholars of the various churches have rendered an invaluable service to the cause of liturgical renewal. They have brought us farther along the path to ecumenical convergence than would have been thought possible fifty years ago. And they have provided a solid foundation for future discussions and research by giving us a clearer picture of the factors that the churches recognize as essential to effective liturgy. These factors have been nicely summarized in the following statement from Geoffrey Wainwright:

> Two guiding stars have been fixed on by the churches in their common search [for convergence in the understanding and practice of the Lord's Supper]: they have attended carefully to the Church of the New Testament and the early centuries, and they have tried to reckon with the social and cultural circumstances of our time. . . . Christian authenticity requires that it be the *original gospel* which is celebrated *in today's world*.[5]

We take our cue from the principles summarized here. On the one hand, liturgy must respond to the recognized foundations of the tradition. That tradition is to be found especially in the New Testament and other documents of the early church. On the other hand, liturgy must also respond to the "social and cultural circumstances of our time." That is to say, in order for liturgy to communicate the principles derived from the tradition, it must be in a form that coheres with the social and cultural experiences and expectations of the people. In this study, we will be providing new perspectives on each of these aspects of liturgy by presenting results from recent research in the New Testament and in the field of ritual studies.

A re-examination of the tradition

Part of the foundation for the tradition is, of course, the New Testament. Indeed, it is often cited as the bedrock foundation when the so-called "words of institution" of Jesus are referred to. Yet the earliest texts that give us clear, unambiguous evidence for early forms of the liturgy are not New Testament texts but those of the church fathers.[6] The New Testament is part of the picture, of course, but it is found to function in the form preserved in the church's traditional interpretation rather than as an independent witness in itself.

When we examine those traditional interpretations in the light of New Testament scholarship, we find that there are significant differences. For example, tradition posits one original event, Jesus' Last Supper, as the basis for all subsequent liturgy. In New Testament scholarship, however, it is widely acnowledged that we cannot reconstruct one version of that event, nor even establish with certainty that there was such an event. Yet these views have not been given their proper place in liturgical discussions. Rather, these discussions have continued to utilize the idea of one origin as part of the foundation for the concept of an orthodox line of tradition.

Furthermore, what we do find in the New Testament is significant variety in the "eucharistic" practices of the New Testament communities. Again, this point has been widely acknowledged, but suppressed in favor of the singular tradition preserved in the later orthodox liturgies. It is true that the tradition provides a record of biblical interpretation in the early church.

The New Testament texts were interpreted in such a way as to support the later forms of liturgy. That traditional interpretation has its own value in the total picture. But to the extent that we in the church today are part of an on-going history of interpretation, we should also allow the text to speak to us anew.

In making this appeal to the New Testament it is not our intention to use a biblicistic argument or call for a return to the "New Testament church". But if, in fact, there has been a "strange silence" of the New Testament witness in liturgical formulations, as we allege, then we need to pay attention to

that point. The New Testament should be allowed to speak
to us on its own terms.

Our analysis suggests that there are significant differences
between the traditional interpretations of the New Testament
witness and what we can determine that the New Testament
actually says. Rather than to singularity, the New Testament
witnesses to a multiplicity of liturgical practices. That
multiplicity reflects the fact that for these churches liturgy
was not seen as a means to preserve a relic from the past but
rather as a dynamic way to address the church of the present.
This interpretation results not in a devaluing but in a "re-
valuing" of the authority of the tradition, for it provides a
model that allows us to value the multiplicity in current
liturgical practice and empowers us to extend liturgical
renewal in more creative directions.

Understanding liturgy today

Our traditional way of looking at liturgy has often limited
our efforts to revitalize it. Liturgy has come to be dominated
by an over-concern for the idea of "orthodoxy" or correct
doctrine. This has tended to produce a sense of liturgy that is
tied to word and emphasizes a narrowed, single line of
tradition. It tends to be a monolithic and rigid view and
creates an environment in which creative interaction with the
culture and the lives of the people is proscribed.

This predisposition towards a particular view of liturgy
has influenced the way in which we have read the ancient
texts. We have read them in terms of the single line of
tradition. We have thus found there only what we were
looking for – warrant for a narrowed sense of correct
doctrine. In the process we may have missed what the texts
really have to tell us.

We have also been hindered by a narrow and negative view
of ritual that is endemic to our culture, especially that aspect
of our culture that is dominated by a traditional Protestant
perspective. That ritual has long been a problem for
Protestant sensibilities is well-known. As the anthropologist
Mary Douglas reminds us:

The long history of Protestantism witnesses to the need for continual watch on the tendency of ritual form to harden and replace religious feeling. In wave upon wave the Reformation has continued to thunder against the empty encrustration of ritual. So long as Christianity has any life, it will never be time to stop echoing the parable of the Pharisee and the Publican, to stop saying that external forms can become empty and mock the truths they stand for. With every new century we become heirs to a longer and more vigorous anti-ritualistic tradition.[7]

Yet, as she goes on to point out, we cannot ignore the importance of ritual:

It is a mistake to suppose that there can be religion which is all interior, with no rules, no liturgy, no external signs of inward states. As with society, so with religion, external form is the condition of its existence . . . As a social animal, man is a ritual animal.[8]

This longstanding perspective in Protestantism has falsely proposed that ritual stand over against true "feeling" in religion, which is then interpreted as an "interior" state over against the "exterior" action that is ritual. What we have missed is the essential relation between "feeling" and exterior action. That is to say, ritual should be seen as an outlet for emotions, even as an enhancement to the emotional involvement of the individual in worship.

On the other hand, an anthropologist like Mary Douglas would insist that there is no such thing as an "empty" ritual. Ritual by its very nature carries meaning. And ritual serves a purpose in our lives as humans that we cannot deny. This perspective gives a clearer focus to our study.

If, as we have said, liturgy today has about it a lifelessness, as if it is a rote repetition of an ancient rite, yet on the other hand we must acnowledge that all liturgy has meaning, how do we reconcile these two positions? The reconciliation is to be sought in a more precise understanding of the message that is being conveyed in our liturgy. We need to be more aware how ritual functions and what the meanings of symbolic language and actions today are. Then when we "read" what we are saying in our contemporary liturgies, we may be surprised to find that we are not saying what we think.

Such an analysis calls for our utilizing new perspectives on our data. For example, we need to give more attention to the insights of ritual studies, in which ritual is analysed on its own terms and interpreted according to its own social referents rather than in terms of official explanations. This perspective allows us to understand what "subliminal" messages, so to speak, are being proclaimed by the ritual process, regardless of the "word" that is spoken. It is a perspective that gives due weight to the power of ritual, a power that taps into the deeper symbolic levels of culture.

This is the perspective that we will seek to apply to our study here. It is a perspective that seeks to place liturgy within its cultural context and understand how it functions as a form of language that is specific to that context. It is a perspective that will be applied to both the ancient and the contemporary data.

This means that we will be working with a definition of "liturgy" and "worship" somewhat different from what might be commonly assumed. For our purposes "worship" will be defined as the totality of word and action that takes place whenever a religious community comes together for an explicit or even implicit religious purpose. "Liturgy" will be used in an equally broad sense, to refer to any separable portion of worship that has particular structure and definition.

The form of liturgy that is given specific focus in this study is that which is traditionally to be related to the Lord's Supper/eucharistic practices of the churches. When we apply the broader view of liturgy as suggested above, this means that we will be casting our net much wider than is tradition-ally done. In our analysis of the New Testament documents we will be looking at the larger phenomenon of meal practices of the early Christian communities. Similarly, when we look at the contemporary scene, we will be looking at a broader definition of the sense of the "Lord's Supper" than is contained in the traditional formal liturgies.

Finally, the "language" that liturgy speaks needs to be reassessed and brought into line with the "social and cultural circumstances of our time." That is to say, liturgy as a form of ritual speaks an aesthetic, symbolic language by means of action as well as word. It is not to be reduced to mere word, as if its meaning were contained totally in written texts.

Indeed, to a great extent the natural ability of liturgy to adjust to new cultural circumstances has been inhibited by the emphasis, especially in Protestant circles, on the word, especially the printed word. When liturgy is circumscribed by the issue of orthodoxy, then it loses contact with the life of the people. It then becomes responsive only to doctrinal concerns and loses that essential interaction between tradition and culture.

Furthermore, the ways in which the social and cultural realities of our time are reflected in liturgy need re-examination as well. In times past, the church drew strength from a lively interaction with the creative geniuses of culture. The great artists in various media – figures such as Michelangelo and Da Vinci, Mozart and Handel, Dante and Goethe – made contributions that represented the highest levels of artistic expression for their day.

Today it seems that the church has become more and more estranged from the creative minds of contemporary culture. Liturgical renewal now belongs to the keepers of right doctrine; the lifeblood of culture, as expressed in the creative arts, has been too often effectively cut off. As a result, we have lost touch with the symbolic language that is expressive of life as it is lived today.

This is not a problem that we can alleviate with this one study alone. But we can make a step toward addressing it. To that end, we have provided here a set of studies that reflect a profound respect for the same principles that have driven liturgical renewal for the past century. On the one hand, we propose a new look at the New Testament data, one that takes seriously the diversity that is there and attempts to account for it as reflective of real issues in the lives of those communities. On the other hand, we propose a new look at the perspective from which we look at liturgy today with a view to understanding better how ritual functions in human societies. Finally, we will present a set of alternative liturgies that attempt to respond to the perspectives developed in these studies.

What we hope to provide is a fresh look at eucharistic renewal. We propose that a new realization of the diverse and dynamic origins of Christian meal traditions can provide a model for renewal of worship today. It can liberate us from old models and point us toward liturgies that are both reflective of the tradition and energized by a creative inter-action with contemporary sensibilities and symbols.

The Greco-Roman Banquet: Defining a Common Meal Tradition

The fact that early Christians regularly ate a meal together when they met as a community is a characteristic that they had in common with virtually every other social group in their world. Furthermore, when these various groups held their meals, they followed similar patterns and rules. This reflects the fact that for the ancients the meal, or more particularly the banquet, was a social institution that was shared in common throughout the culture regardless of the social or ethnic distinctiveness that a group might otherwise have.

When we study ancient meals from this perspective, it means that we no longer consider each type of meal as a separate entity, but rather understand them as manifestations of a common tradition. Thus the pattern for ancient meals can be diagrammed like this:

Common	→	Adapted	= family gatherings
			= funerary banquets
meal	→	to various	= sacrificial banquets
			= philosophical society meetings
tradition	→	settings	= trade guild meetings
			= religious society meetings
			= Jewish festival meals
			= Christian meals

It should be noted that the same basic patterns were present whether the meal is to be designated "secular" or "sacred". On the one hand, there was a religious component to every "secular" meal. On the other hand, every "sacred" banquet was also a social occasion. Some meals might have placed a greater emphasis on the religious component because of an enhanced religious function or setting, but the form and ideology still derived from the common meal tradition.

This is the social context in which early Christian meal practices developed in form and function; Christian meals were not significantly different from those in their culture. It is therefore important that we understand the nature of the common meal tradition in order better to interpret early Christian meals. What is here designated as the "common meal tradition" is the tradition of the Greco-Roman banquet, which was a complex and important social institution in the ancient world. It can be seen as the primary carrier of meal tradition in the ancient world.

One way in which the common meal tradition can be traced is by noting the pattern of the adoption of the custom of reclining at formal meals by the various peoples of the Mediterranean world. Greeks, Romans, and Jews had traditions that their people once sat at meals before taking up the custom of reclining. This custom seems to have originated in the Eastern Mediterranean world and was known to the Jewish people as early as the eighth century BCE (Amos 6:4–7). The Greeks appear to have adopted the custom from the Assyrians and were practicing it as early as the sixth century BCE.[1] The Romans soon followed suit. Since reclining tended to carry with it other meal conventions and since Greeks, Romans, and Jews were interacting culturally in many ways in this period, their meal customs also soon came to be standardized and shared in common.

In the Jewish data for the New Testament period, our evidence indicates that reclining was the normal posture for formal meals. This tradition is represented in the passover liturgy in the Mishnah, a text that can be dated to the third century but may reflect tradition from the first century or earlier. Here reclining is specifically mentioned as a require-ment at this festival meal (*Mishnah Pesahim* 10:1), an unusual notation which would suggest that it was a custom that derived from an earlier period but was no longer the norm for the later period. In the Gospels, whenever a posture at table is indicated for the meals of Jesus, it is always reclining.

A reclining meal would usually be the evening meal or banquet, which was the meal that tended to have the most formalities connected with it. If a meal was to be used as a special occasion for a social gathering of friends or family or for a meeting of a club or religious group, it would normally be the evening meal. Thus the formal evening meal, or banquet, is the one to which the most elaborate traditions and rules of etiquette became attached.

Features of banquet customs

The norm in the ancient world, like today, was that an individual would host a banquet in his house for his friends and associates. Ancient houses in fact gave pride of place to the dining room as the most elaborate and highly decorated, because it was the room where guests would be entertained. On some occasions, however, a banquet might be held in another location. Banquet facilities were provided for general use (by citizens only, of course) in various public buildings in the normal Greek city, including temple complexes. Paul refers to the convention of taking meals at a temple as a custom practiced by members of the Christian community at Corinth (1 Corinthians 8:10).

Invitations were extended to the guests in advance of the meal, as indicated, for example, in Sirach 13:9. In some cases, it would appear that this was done in oral form, as was the case in Xenophon's *Symposium* 1.2–7. We also have examples of formal written invitations. One group of papyrus invita-tions deriving from Egypt and dated from the second to the fourth centuries CE utilizes a standard form, as illustrated in the following examples:

Dioscoros invites you to dine at the wedding of her son on the 14th of Mesore in the temple of Sabazius from the ninth hour, Farewell.

Diogenes invites you to dinner for the first birthday of his daughter in the Serapeum tomorrow which is Pachon 26 from the eighth hour onwards.[2]

Also notable in these examples is the fact that they refer to "secular" meals being held at temple locations. This is further evidence for the perspective also exhibited by Paul in 1 Corinthians 8:10, that people often utilized the dining facilities at temples for non-religious purposes, much as we might utilize a church fellowship hall for a civic meeting today.

Dining rooms were furnished with couches for the diners to recline. There were various traditional styles and arrangements of couches as indicated in both the archaeological and literary evidence. It was expected, however, that regardless of the arrangement there was a ranking assigned to the positions. Thus each guest would be placed according to his status in relation to that of the other guests. Ranking the guests appropriately could be a tricky procedure for the hosts, and embarrassing situations and social gaffes are commonplace in the literature. Plutarch, for example, makes use of this common motif when he refers to a situation in which a distinguished guest arrived late to a banquet and, not finding a position available worth of his rank, left angrily (*Table Talk*, 615D). The same motif is utilized in a parable of Jesus as recorded by Luke, a parable which warns against taking a "place on honor" at the table lest a higher-ranking guest arrive later and claim that position (Luke 14:7–11).

Normally, the ranking order started at the highest position and continued around the room to the right to the lowest position. It was also customary for diners to share couches, as is indicated both in the literature and in vase paintings of Greek banquets. The vase paintings show diners reclining parallel to one another on their left sides and eating with their right hands. These features of the dining customs aid us in interpreting the reference in John to the disciple who dined "lying close to the breast of Jesus" (13:23) or the reference in the parable of the Rich Man and Lazarus to the position of Lazarus after death in "Abraham's bosom" (Luke 16:22). In both cases, the reference is to the individual who reclines to the right of the host or guest of honor and thus has an honored position at the table. In the Lukan parable, therefore, the reference alludes to a symbolic representation of the blessings of the afterlife as being like a festive banquet.

It was customary for the household servant to wash the feet of the guests before they reclined, as indicated, for example, in Plato's *Symposium*: "So the attendant washed him and made him ready for reclining" (175A). The same custom is referred to in the Lukan story where Jesus dines at the home of a Pharisee. Here the Pharisee is accused of a major insult by not having provided for the washing of his guest's feet (Luke 7:44). When Jesus washes the feet of the disciples in John's version of the Last Supper, he is, of course, symbolically taking on the role of a servant (John 13:1–11).

Washing the hands before the meal was also a normal part of Greco-Roman banquet customs. This is alluded to in a reference in Athenaeus, "water over the hand, tables brought in" (14.641d), in which the bringing in of the tables refers to the serving of the food. This custom was elevated to religious ritual in Judaism as indicated in the Mishnah (*Hagigah* 2:5) and in the references in the Gospels (as in Mark 7:3), where this is a point of dispute between Jesus and the Pharisees.

There were two major courses in a banquet, the *deipnon* ("supper" or "banquet"), which was the meal proper, followed by the *symposion* ("symposium"), which was the drinking party. This form is reflected in the Lord's Supper traditions in the New Testament in which the wine is drunk "after supper [*deipnon*]" (Luke 22:20; 1 Corinthians 11:25). In some cases there was also an appetizer course at the beginning of the meal (Athenaeus 2.58b–60b). This custom is reflected in our earliest Jewish passover liturgy, in which an appetizer course precedes the main course ("When they bring him the food, he dips the lettuce in vinegar before he comes to the breaking of the bread," *Mishnah Pesahim* 10:3).

The end of the first course and the beginning of the second was marked off by special rituals, beginning with the removal of the tables and the bringing in of the wine bowl for mixing the wine. The proportion of water to wine varied, but common mixtures were five parts water to two parts wine or three parts water to one part wine (Athenaeus 10.426d). The beginning of the symposium would then be marked by the offering of a libation to the gods and other religious ceremonies, such as the singing of a hymn. This ritual is referred to in Plato's *Symposium* 176A:

> After this, it seems, when Socrates had taken his place and had dined with the rest, they made libation and sang a chant to the god and so forth, as custom bids, till they betook them to drinking.

In Judaism, there developed a traditional benediction over the wine: "For over wine he says, 'Blessed are you, O Lord, our God, King of the Universe, Creator of the fruit of the vine'" (*Mishnah Berakhot* 6:1). In essence, it is the same custom as that of the Greeks but offered to a different deity. Early Christian groups probably used a similar benediction, especially since they prayed to the same God, and in one case, in 1 Corinthians 10:16, the wine ceremony is referred to with a Jewish phrase "cup of blessing." There was not yet, however, a standard benediction for either Jews or Christians.

The second course or symposium was a time for extended leisurely drinking of wine accompanied by the entertainment of the evening. There were various traditional forms of symposium entertainment. Some would fit our definition of "party games," such as the popular game of *kottabos* in which a contest would be held to see who could most accurately fling the last drops of wine in his cup into a wine bowl at the center of the room. Other forms of entertainment would include various kinds of musical, dance, and dramatic presentations, such as the entertainment provided at the symposium of Socrates as described by Xenophon in which a dance was performed enacting the erotic encounter of Dionysus and Ariadne on their wedding night (*Symposium* 9.2–7). Dramatic enactments of mythological stories were also utilized as entertainment at the banquets of religious associations, in which case they would serve a special "religious" function analogous to what we might identify as a "liturgical" function. An example is found in the statutes of the Iobakchoi, a Bacchic club in which specifications for various "roles" to be played at the banquet meeting include deities and other mythological characters (lines 124–25).[3] Besides these forms of formal entertainment, symposia were also famous for other forms of "entertainment" as well, in which erotic liaisons with one's couch-mates or with the flute girl were evidently not uncommon.

In the philosophical tradition of the symposium, there developed a motif in which the entertainment of the evening would be devoted to elevated conversation appropriate to a convivial gathering of philosophers. This tradition was especially built on the precedent established in Plato's *Symposium* (176E):

> "Since it has been resolved, then," said Eryximachus, "that we are to drink only so much as each desires, with no constraint on any, I next propose that the flute-girl who came in just now be dismissed: let her pipe to herself or, if she likes, to the women-folk within, but let us seek our entertainment today in conversation."

It is this tradition that becomes the most distinctive feature of the philosophical symposium both in its literary form and in the actual practice in so much as we can reconstruct it.

This tradition becomes one of the most important features of the symposium that is adapted for use in Jewish and Christian communities. A meal of a Jewish sage with his disciples, for example, could take on a form similar to that of a meal of a philosopher with his disciples. Just as the philosophical group would discuss a topic of significance to their school of thought, so also the circle of the sage would discuss the Torah (Sirach 9:14–15; *Mishnah Abot* 3.3). So also

the Jewish sect known as the Therapeutae were said by Philo
to have engaged in discourse on the meaning of the law (*On
the Contemplative Life* 75–79). Similarly, while the meetings at
table of the early Christians are still somewhat obscure to us,
there are indications that instruction took place at table (see
Acts 20:7). Consistent with this interpretation is the face that
the Gospel communities prefer to idealize Jesus as teaching at
table (see specially Luke 14).

Forms of banquets

When an individual wished to get together with his friends or
business or religious associates, he would generally do so by
inviting them to his home for a banquet. Banquets were also
held on important family occasions, such as birthdays,
weddings, and funerals. Plutarch and Lucian, for example,
place philosophical banquets in the context of birthday and
wedding feasts, references which indicate at the least that
such celebrations were common (see Plutarch *Table Talk*
717B; Lucian, *Symposium* 5). Wedding banquets are also
featured in the Gospels, particularly as a motif in the parables
(as in Matthew 22:2; Luke 12:36; 14:8) and in the famous
scene in Cana in John 2:1–11. Banquets were also the usual
means for celebrating religious festivals, which were
common in both pagan religion and in Judaism.

Various kinds of organized clubs also met for communal
meals, and sometimes seem to have been organized almost
exclusively for the purpose of providing banquets for their
members from a common purse. We know of various kinds
of such clubs, especially from inscriptions which provide
records of their official business and often define the rules for
their banquets.[4] One type of club could be called a trade
guild, since it was made up of individuals who had the same
occupation. Their purpose, however, was to provide a social
outlet rather than a political lobby. Sometimes they would
also keep a fund to provide appropriate burial rituals for their
members. In this respect they were similar to another type of
club, the funerary societies, which were organized solely for
that purpose. Since ancient funeral rites included banquets in

honor of the dead, the meetings of these groups were dedicated especially to memorial meals on the occasions of funerals or anniversaries of funerals of their deceased members and patrons. Organizations like these especially attracted individuals of modest income, since they provided social occasions, as well as the promise of a relatively elaborate funeral, that would not otherwise be accessible to them.

Greco-Roman clubs of all types often had patron deities. Some of them, however, were organized for the purpose of honoring a patron deity. We refer to these as religious societies. They often met in quarters provided at the sanctuary of the deity, or in their own clubhouse, which provided facilities for religious rituals. Their meetings were also primarily banquet meetings, but often included a more pronounced religious component.

There were also many philosophical schools which met for communal meals. The philosophical tradition, of course, is especially associated with the classic definition of the symposium. This tradition goes back at least to Plato and the literary form which he helped to popularize, whereby a meal of philosophers would be described, with an emphasis on the philosophical dialogue that would take place during the drinking party. This is known as the literary form of the symposium, and became highly influential whenever any literary reference was made to meals, whether real or imaginary. It was also influential in Jewish and Christian literature, as seen for example in the Jewish *Letter of Aristeas* and in various sections of the New Testament where meals are referred to, such as in the Gospel of Luke.[5]

Various religious sectarian groups had a formal organization similar to that of the clubs and also centered many of their meetings upon meals. The Jewish groups known as the Essenes of Qumran and the Therapeutae, which were found in Egypt, were especially known for their communal meals. In both cases, the meal served as an important occasion for affirmation of community identity and values. Participation in the meal was tantamount to membership in the community. Thus for the Essenes there was an extensive process of purification involved before one would be allowed to partake of the "common food" (Josephus, *The Jewish War* 2, 138–9).

The early Christian groups were a similar form of Jewish sect, especially to the extent that they defined their community boundaries differently from those of Judaism as a whole. They, too, centered their meetings on communal meals. Their structure was so much like that of the Greco-Roman clubs that they were taken to be a form of club, especially when a legal definition of the Christian movement was sought, as was the case when Pliny defined them as a "political association" on the basis of their gatherings for communal meals (Pliny, *Letters* 10.96). The same was true of certain of the other Jewish sects. In this the officials were probably not far wrong, since these groups probably did imitate many of the organizational features of the clubs, only changing the identity of the patron deity.

Banquet ideology

The importance of meal customs and etiquette as an aspect of culture has been given a great deal of attention in recent anthropological studies. A leader in this research is Mary Douglas, who has analysed meals in both ancient and modern cultures. Her studies call our attention to the fact that religion and its component parts, myth and ritual, cannot be properly understood except in relation to the larger culture as a whole.

Douglas' insights into meals are nicely summarized in this statement:

> If food is treated as a code, the messages it encodes will be found in the pattern of social relations being expressed. The message is about different degrees of hierarchy, inclusion and exclusion, boundaries and transactions across the boundaries. Like sex, the taking of food has a social component, as well as a biological one.[6]

Similar observations can be made about the Greco-Roman data. Here also meals represent a "social code" which expresses patterns of social relations. These features make up what can be called the ideology of the banquet. It can be seen in the function of meals in defining groups and their values. This is especially accessible to us in the various discussions of proper behavior or etiquette at meals. For here we find appeal being made to the idealized form a meal should take.

The patterns of social relations that make up ancient banquet ideology may be categorized as follows:

1. Social bonding

This refers to the phenomenon whereby the meal creates a special tie among the diners. Indeed, the meal became the primary means for celebrating and enhancing community ties. This is seen in the fact that not only was it the chief social activity of various groups of comrades or acquaintances, but it also tended to be the central, if not the only, group activity of the various clubs and associations in the Greek and Roman world. As Mary Douglas points out, banquets served to define boundaries between various groups. Plutarch refers to the power of this imagery when he refers to "the friend-making character of the table" (*Table Talk* 614A–B). This imagery, in fact, is widespread in the ancient literature, so that "friendship" becomes especially associated with the bonds created at the table. In the New Testament, it is notable that Jesus is defined as a "friend of tax collectors and sinners" precisely by his act of dining with them.

2. Social obligation

The fact that a meal created a special tie among the diners in turn led to an ethical obligation of each to the other. For the Greeks, what we moderns refer to as "etiquette" was included as a significant category of social ethics. Indeed, there developed an extensive tradition of philosophical discussion of "symposium laws" in which etiquette was included under important ethical categories such as "friendship," "love," "joy," or "pleasure." These were defined not as individual but as group values, so that individual behavior would come under the rubric of that which served the goal of friendship or pleasure of the group as a whole. Such discussions became a stock feature of philosophy, from Plato and Aristotle to Plutarch, and were quite influential in later developments of meal ideology.

The form which these discussions often took concerned ways in which behavior was defined to serve the common good. Quarreling or abusive behavior was not allowed at club meetings, for example, because it did not serve the goal of the "good cheer" of all. Indeed, "factions" of any kind at a meal were out of order. The by-laws of the Guild of Zeus Hypsistos, for example, forbade making "factions" (line 13),[7] as did Paul in his instructions to the Corinthian Christians (1 Corinthians 11:17–34). In Sirach, the Jewish sage devoted an extensive section to meal etiquette under the rubric, "Judge your neighbor's feelings by your own, and in every matter be thoughtful" (Sirach 31:15).

Conversation at the symposium was also addressed by these rules. Thus Plutarch counseled that a conversation at table should be one in which all can participate (*Table Talk* 614E). So also Paul argued that "conversation" at Christian gatherings, meetings which evidently began with a meal together (1 Corinthians 11:17–34), should be conducted in such a way that they "edified" the group as a whole; thus each should speak in turn rather than in a disorderly fashion (1 Corinthians 14:26–33).

3. Social stratification

Those who dined at the ancient table were always aware of their differing social rankings. For example, the act of reclining in itself indicated rank, for it was traditionally the posture reserved for free citizens and prohibited to women, children, and slaves. In Xenophon's *Symposium*, for example, the youth Autolycus sits next to his father who reclines, even though the banquet is given in his honor (1.8). Even when the custom was relaxed somewhat during the Roman period and women began to recline along with the men, the old "social code" continued to be attached to it. Thus, in a satirical description of a fictitious philosophical banquet at which women are present and evidently reclining, Lucian relates how it had become so crowded that there was no more room for a late-arriving guest to stretch out on one of the couches. He is therefore invited to sit rather than recline. He angrily refuses, however, and chooses to recline on the floor, on the grounds that sitting at table is "womanish and weak" (*Symposium* 13). The same "social code" is evidently being addressed in the Jewish passover liturgy found in the Mishnah, for it specified that even the poor are to "recline" at this meal: "And even the poorest Israelite should not eat until he reclines at his table" (*Pesahim* 10.1).

Another way in which social stratification was present at the banquet was in the practice of ranking the guests by their position at table. To honor a person's social rank was considered appropriate and was defended according to the ethical argument that it was a sign of the "good order" that should characterize a banquet. Besides placement at table, an individual's social rank could also be indicated by other means, such as the quality or quantity of food he was given.

Various clubs and social organizations utilized this custom to designate rank within the group. Thus club officers would be designated assigned places at table and special portions in the distribution of meat. So also the placement of individuals at the communal meal of the Essenes at Qumran was specified according to their rank in the community (*Rule of the Congregation* [1QSa] 2.11–22).

4. Social equality

At the same time that social rankings of the guests were assumed, so also there was a sense of social equality among the diners as well. This idea seemed to work in constant tension with that of social stratification and can be seen as an elaboration of the idea of social bonding. From this perspective there developed the view that the meal tended to break down social barriers. It is a theme that is found as early as Homer, where "equal banquets" are said to characterize the dining habits of the heroes (*Iliad* 1.468,602; 2.431; etc.), and as late as the second century, where "equal privilege" at the table is promised to the worshippers of Zeus Panamoros.[8] It is not always clear what is meant by the term "equal," since it does not necessarily rule out the customary perquisites of one's rank, but that some sense of equality was a strong part of the "social code" of meals is nevertheless apparent.

This theme crops up at various points in the data. A reference in Plutarch is especially instructive. He refers to a banquet where the group agreed to forego the normal ranking at table and each recline where he wished. In the accompanying conversation, such equality at the meal is argued for as an inherent aspect of banquet "friendship." According to this line of argument, the diners should leave behind the divisive social rankings of outer society and in effect form a new society with new social rules when they entered the door of the dining chamber (*Table Talk* 616C–F).

It should be noted that this argument in Plutarch is included among several others, one of which argues for the orderliness of ranking and against the anarchy that is to be associated with an abolition of ranking (*Table Talk* 615E–616B). This is illustrative of the curious way in which meals communicated both equality and hierarchy and kept them in constant tension. Philo reflects this when he notes that at the table of the Therapeutae "equality" rules, since there are no slaves and women recline along with men, albeit in a separate section of the room. Yet at the same meal there is ranking according to seniority (*On the Contemplative Life* 67–72). The equality that lies at the heart of the ideal communal meal is also reflected in the passover liturgy specification that the poor should also recline equally at table on this occasion and receive at least four cups of wine ("And even the poorest Israelite should not eat until he reclines at his table. And they should provide him with no fewer than four cups of wine, and even if the funds come from public charity," *Mishnah Pesahim* 10.1), although this does not rule out the possibility that higher ranking participants at the meal might receive more.

From Greco-Roman banquet to Christian banquet

This complex banquet tradition explains why various early Christian groups appear to have centered their meetings upon fellowship meals. That is to say, the evidence suggests that any social group that came into existence in the ancient world would commonly celebrate communal meals together. This factor offers adequate explanation for the phenomenon of communal meals in early Christian groups and indeed helps explain the fact that, while meals were common in early Christianity, interpretations of these meals varied. It furthermore provides the basis for the development of the "ideology" connected with their meals. That is to say, the Greco-Roman banquet provided both the form and the basic ideology for the development of early Christian meal liturgy.

· 3 ·

The New Testament Banquet: Improvising on a Common Theme

When you meet together, it is not the Lord's supper that you eat. For in eating, each one goes ahead with his own meal, and one is hungry and another is drunk (1 Corinthians 11:20–21).

The reference to the Christian meal in 1 Corinthians is one of our only texts that describes such an occasion with any detail whatsoever. When we look closely at the kind of occasion it was, it is clear that it was a complete meal, and one which was structured according to the normal pattern of an ancient banquet. This is indicated not only by the reference in the text quoted above to food and drink sufficient for drunkenness and allaying of hunger, but also to the terminology itself. For it is "after the *deipnon* (supper)" that the wine blessing is spoken (11:25). This fits the normal format for the Greco–Roman banquet in which the second course, which was devoted to the drinking of wine, followed the first course, which was the meal proper.

This text provides explicit evidence for the thesis of this chapter, that early Christian meals were all variations of the Greco–Roman banquet and should be studied from that perspective. For when we apply to the evidence the model of the Greco–Roman banquet, we are able to understand much more clearly how the banquet functioned as the centerpiece of early Christian worship and liturgy.

This perspective represents a revision of the traditional understanding of the development of the early Christian eucharist. Earlier studies approached the history of the eucharist from the perspective of the codified forms that developed in the later centuries and led to standardized liturgies.[1] Thus the first-century evidence tended to be condensed down to that which could be seen to be the predecessor to the "orthodox" liturgies. When seen through this lens, the first-century data is made to take on the appearance of a single line of tradition. This approach does not, however, do justice to the variety that we find in the data.

A more fruitful approach is one that recognizes the origins of the meal practices of the early Christians in the social institution of the banquet which they shared with their culture. This approach accounts for the variety we find in the data and helps us to analyze what it all means. This perspective can be diagrammed as follows:

Common	→	Multiple		Collapsed
	→	social		into
Meal	→	settings	→	orthodox
	→	= multiple		liturgies
Tradition	→	meals		

From common meal tradition, therefore, different groups developed variations in the form and interpretation of their meals. What is apparently at work is an adaptation of the common banquet tradition to fit specific needs and situations. This means first of all that there was not a consciousness of a single authoritative tradition where it all began. This idea is already apparent in Paul, who refers to a Jesus tradition but adapts it for his own purposes. Second, the variations nevertheless represent recognizable adaptations of the common banquet tradition. Third, the variations also represent responses to individual social situations. The principles by which early developments in liturgy were taking place, therefore, is that communities were responding ritually to their social situations and doing so by utilizing meal traditions common to their culture. In order to illustrate this principle at work we will now look at representative examples from the New Testament.

The Last Supper tradition

The New Testament meal that has been the focus of most attention is that of the Last Supper of Jesus. This tradition is found in several versions in the New Testament. Most of these texts center on specific blessings spoken over the bread and the wine at a meal that is described as the last Jesus ate with his disciples on the evening before he died. This setting for the meal is mirrored in the blessings themselves, in which allusions are made to the upcoming death of Jesus and how it is to be interpreted. In a narrative tradition that evidently originates with Mark, the meal is further identified as a passover meal (Mark 14:12–16). A separate tradition in Paul identifies this text as somehow providing a model for early Christian meals ("Do this . . .," 1 Corinthians 11:24, 25).

These are the bare facts of the data. In order to assess this tradition correctly, however, we should note in detail the form in which it has come down to us. For example, it must be emphasized that while these events are placed in a historical framework, they are not presented as historical reminiscences *per se*. That is to say, like all texts in the Jesus tradition, they are here because they are perceived to have specific meanings to early Christian communities. It is these meanings that are most accessible to us and, furthermore, are most important for our study. Our goal is to understand better how early Christians practiced and interpreted their community meals. The Last Supper texts must therefore be seen in terms of their functions in these communities.

There are at least four versions of the Last Supper tradition preserved in our texts. Although they all share in placing the meal on the evening before Jesus died, they differ significantly in their details, so much so that they appear to attest to independent traditions. Three versions, namely those of Paul, Mark, and Luke, place the emphasis on the so-called "eucharistic sayings of Jesus."[2] The fourth version is in John 13:1–11. Here there is no reference to the tradition of eucharistic sayings at all. Rather, the emphasis is on the ritual of footwashing at the meal.

Of the three versions of the eucharistic sayings, Luke's is the latest and most complex. It combines elements of Mark and Paul along with independent materials. Because of textual variations, Luke has what is called a "long text" version (22:15–20) and a "short text" version (omits 19b–20). The "long text" version has sayings connected with a cup, bread, then a second cup; the "short text" has a cup saying followed by a bread saying. Both text traditions, therefore, present versions of the Last Supper that are different from those of Mark and Paul.

The versions of Paul and Mark are the earliest accounts of the eucharistic sayings of Jesus and are usually the texts on which theories of origins of the eucharist are based. These two basic texts are as follows:

> For I received from the Lord what I also delivered to you, that the Lord Jesus on the night when he was arrested [RSV: betrayed] took bread, and when he had given thanks, he broke it, and said, "This is my body which is for you. Do this in remembrance of me." In the same way also the cup, after supper, saying, "This cup is the new covenant in my blood. Do this, as often as you drink it, in remembrance of me." For as often as you eat this bread and drink the cup, you proclaim the Lord's death until he comes (1 Corinthians 11:23–26).

> And as they were eating, he took bread, and blessed, and broke it, and gave it to them, and said, "Take; this is my body." And he took a cup, and when he had given thanks he gave it to them, and they all drank of it. And he said to them, "This is my blood of the covenant, which is poured out for many. Truly, I say to you, I shall not drink again of the fruit of the vine until that day when I drink it new in the kingdom of God." (Mark 14:22–25)

It is clear that these two versions differ in major details, as
has often been pointed out in previous scholarship.[3] For
example, the bread-saying in Paul has an interpretation
attached to the metaphor of "body"; the saying in Mark does
not. The cup-saying in Paul equates the sharing of cup with
covenant which is ratified by blood. The saying in Mark
equates the content, the wine, with blood which is interpreted both in terms of covenant and martyrdom. Only in
Paul is there a command to repeat the ceremony, and it is
connected with the theme of memorial. In Mark, on the
other hand, the text is enclosed in a narrative context, just as
are the other Jesus stories, without any obvious sense that it is
intended to mirror liturgical practices in the Markan
community, or, if it is, how it is to do so.

There are thus major problems involved in interpreting
these texts as references either to a historical event or to a
single liturgical tradition. The first problem, of course, is that
the texts do not agree. Thus any proposal that would attempt
to identify an original event behind these texts would have to
ao so on the basis of a reconstruction rather than on a literal
reading of the texts.

Many attempts have been made to reconstruct an original
historical event lying behind these texts.[4] The presupposition
behind all such reconstructions is that Jesus in some way
foresaw his death and provided an interpretation of its
meaning through a creative use of benedictions over the
bread and wine. All such presuppositions must, of course, be
weighed against the assessment of Jesus as a human rather
than divine being; while the tradition makes him into a divine
figure, for whom premonitions would be expected, such
characteristics can hardly be applied to a historical figure.

Thus while it may certainly be possible that Jesus had some
premonition that his life was being threatened, the text
moves well beyond normal expectations. Here Jesus not only
knows what will happen, but he has already applied a
meaning to it and ritualized it into a highly complex
theological form. Not only does this strain historical
credulity, but it does not fit what tradition tells us about the

history of the Jesus group immediately after his death. Here tradition asserts that Jesus' death was a surprise and a major blow to their morale. If they had entertained ideas that he was the Messiah, his death would have abolished such thoughts, for the Messiah was supposed to deliver Israel rather than die an ignominious death. Rather than witnessing to a smooth transition for which Jesus' followers were prepared, the tradition instead witnesses to a period of confusion and reassessment. That period of reassessment produced the early theologizing about the meaning of the life and death of Jesus. But the eucharistic sayings texts present a rather advanced stage of that theologizing, since the death has here been given a sophisticated and complex interpretation utilizing a variety of biblical and ritual motifs and symbols. Consequently, it is highly unlikely that one could reconstruct a credible historical event based on the eucharistic sayings texts. Even if one attempted to do so, it is not likely that it would contain sufficient form and content on which an early Christian meal liturgy could be founded.[5]

Indeed, the tradition does not support the view that the Last Supper tradition derives from any hypothetical single original event, whether that event be located in the life of Jesus or in the life of the early church. Note, for example, that the tradition is quite fluid. There are not only various versions, as pointed out above, but also a variety of models for the kind of focus the meal might have had. Was it primarily a memorial meal, on the model of the funerary banquet ("Do this in remembrance of me. ... As often as you eat this bread and drink the cup, you proclaim the Lord's death")? If so, was the theme of the death of the martyr an inherent part of the memorial theme or a separate theme ("This is my body which is for you")? Or was it a covenant meal, perhaps structured on the model of a club banquet ("This cup is the new covenant in my blood/This is my blood of the covenant")? Or was it dominated by the theme of the eschatological banquet ("Truly, I say to you, I shall not drink again of the fruit of the vine until that day when I drink it new in the kingdom of God")? This text tradition exhibits multiplicity rather than singularity. It appears that it was subject to a variety of usages and interpretations throughout the history of its transmission.

We might also note the nature of this text tradition, for in form it can be called an "etiological legend."[6] That is to say, it has taken this shape not as a record of a past event but as a means for explaining the origin and meaning of current practices in the community. Yet there is a certain dissonance between the form of the text tradition and the ritual practices it purports to mirror, for it only speaks of a meal presided over by Jesus; it does not specifically define how it is to function in a liturgical context.

For example, does this tradition assume that someone in the community is to perform the role of Jesus and enact the event, thus saying the words of Jesus as he is said to have s oken them? This would fit a pattern exemplified in the statutes of the religious association known as the Iobakchoi. Here we find an allusion to a liturgical drama performed at their banquets in which members of the club played the roles of divine beings.[7] Or does this text assume that someone would speak words similar to but not equivalent to the text, so as to avoid playing the part of Jesus in the ritual? Or would it have functioned as a reminiscence, to be brought to mind during the celebration of the meal, much as the "etiological legend" of the deliverance of Israel from bondage in Egypt was recounted at the celebration of the passover meal? The text tradition is simply not clear on this point.

Questions like these bring to our attention the fact that the text tradition of the euchariastic sayings of Jesus does not provide a liturgical script. That is to say, it does not specify what prayers are to be spoken, as does, for example, a text like Didache 9–10. At best, it may be seen to provide a model whereby certain specific interpretations would be utilized when the blessings were spoken over the bread and wine. But even if this is the case, there is not a sense of an authoritative interpretation, for it is still attracting new interpretations, namely those of Paul, Mark, Luke, and others, whenever we come across this tradition in our literature.

Furthermore, whatever relation this text tradition may
have had to an actual liturgical event, it must be realized that
it was only part of the furniture, so to speak. It does not
describe the event in its totality. In this sense, it may be
compared to the passover liturgy in the Mishnah (*Pesahim*
10.1–9), a text which *does* come to be viewed as a script. Here
the written text gives us an outline of things to be said and
interpretations to be applied, but the event is not reducible to
this script, as anyone who has attended a Jewish passover can
testify. The event is a festive meal, with all the attendant
meanings that such meals carry. Within that context, certain
specific interpretations are applied according to the outline
text in the Mishnah. Similarly, when the Last Supper
tradition is specifically connected with meal celebration in the
early church, namely in 1 Corinthians 11:17–34, it can be
seen at best to function as a reference to themes and perhaps
specific blessings. The event to which it refers, however, is
the "Lord's Supper," which is a festive banquet, an event
with much greater complexity and breadth of meaning than
is attested by the outline provided by the Last Supper
tradition alone.

A final point is that the Last Supper tradition does not
witness to all the meal traditions and practices in the early
church. As we will see in the analysis below, there are other
meal traditions in the early church that refer neither to the
Last Supper tradition nor to the idea that the meal is a
commemoration of the death of Jesus.

The conclusion to be drawn, therefore, is that our data
does not witness to a single origin or singular meaning for
early Christian meals. Rather, the meal apparently came to
exist as a center of communal self-identity based on its own
inherent meaning in the culture. It needed no further
justification. Various communities then applied differing
interpretations to their meals utilizing various models and
traditions, including the tradition of the Last Supper of Jesus.
But in doing so they were not referring to an authoritative
command or model; that simply does not exist in our data.
The early Christian communities exhibit a great deal of

creativity in their adaptations of meal tradition to fit their own special social situations.

Jesus as "glutton and drunkard" and "friend of tax collectors and sinners"

One early tradition that contains significant data about early Christian meals is the following from the document known as Q. Here, in a context in which Jesus is being contrasted with John the Baptist, there is a harsh criticism by Jesus' enemies of his eating habits.

> To what then shall I compare the men of this generation, and what are they like? They are like children sitting in the market place and calling to one another, "We piped to you, and you did not dance; we wailed, and you did not weep." For John the Baptist has come eating no bread and drinking no wine; and you say, "He has a demon." The Son of Man has come eating and drinking; and you say, "Behold, a glutton and a drunkard, a friend of tax collectors and sinners!" Yet wisdom is justified by all her children (Luke 7:31–35 $\frac{1}{2}$ Matthew 11:16–20).

Two separate traditions are combined here. The first is made up of a contrast between Jesus and John. While John practices an "ascetic" lifestyle, Jesus attends banquets. The second tradition adds another bit of data to the description of Jesus that is not paralleled in the description of John. According to this tradition, Jesus is also in the habit of dining with questionable characters.

The "social code" represented in the first tradition is that meal habits can represent lifestyle in a larger sense, and that the choice of lifestyle can be seen to function as a part of the total message of the teacher. Furthermore, the contrast between the two lifestyles is basic to the meaning, for attending banquets in itself would not stand out. What makes it stand out is when it is viewed in relation to an opposite lifestyle that comes from the same camp. For Jesus and John are seen to represent two aspects of the same message; they are both "wisdom's children," who stand together over against "this generation." The contrast they represent is between the polar opposites, feasting and fasting.

The "social code" represented in the second tradition is the idea of "social bonding" as defined in Chapter 2. According to this idea, social bonds are created when people dine together. This bonding is often referred to under the category of "friendship." So also here, Jesus is seen to be creating bonds of friendship simply by the practice of dining with certain individuals. What stands out here is that the types of individuals mentioned are not those Jesus is expected to dine with. The idea is that Jesus does this purposefully and regularly – it is not an accident – and thus he intends it to have a meaning consistent with his overall message.

This text provides data for at least two levels of the Jesus tradition. It has been widely interpreted as representing a tradition of the historical Jesus. In its present form, however, it is clearly a product of the early Jesus movement. Therefore it also provides information about the form and function of meals in the Q community.

1. The meals of Jesus

This tradition has been widely interpreted as historical. The argument of Norman Perrin can be regarded as representative. He argues that these critiques of Jesus, that he was "a glutton and a drunkard" and that he ate with "tax collectors and sinners," are so outlandish that it is difficult to imagine them originating in the early church. He therefore concludes that they are historical. He interprets this to mean that Jesus ate meals with individuals who were outcasts in Jewish society. "Sinners" qualified as outcasts because they were ritually impure and "tax collectors" because they were "quislings" or collaborators with the Roman government. By dining with them, Jesus was utilizing the meal to symbolize that he was welcoming these individuals into the kingdom. Furthermore, Perrin goes on to argue that Jesus' meal practices function as the best explanation for the fact that early Christians celebrated meals together.[8]

We no longer find these arguments persuasive. On the one

hand, adequate explanation for the early Christian practice of celebrating meals together can be provided by understanding how meals functioned in the culture, as has already been pointed out. On the other hand, this reconstruction of events in Jesus' lifetime takes a lot for granted. A major point is the assumption that Jesus was engaged in establishing a community with a separate identity within the world of Judaism. While this view is still held by a number of scholars, we find it to be highly questionable. It assumes that Jesus took a critical stance over against the Judaism of his day and, further, that he set about establishing an alternative religious organization.

These developments did take place, but are more likely to be located at the level of the Jesus movement that resulted after his death. This is indicated by, among other things, the fact that the early groups did not define themselves as separate from Judaism. On the contrary, they began as movements within Judaism whose eventual separation came about as a result of conflicts that left painful scars. A more likely scenario for the historical Jesus, then, is that he functioned as a teacher within Judaism, most likely connected with the wisdom tradition, whose teachings spawned a movement after his death.

Nevertheless, the idea that Jesus could be characterized as one who preferred banquets, in contrast to John the Baptist, has much to commend it. The preference of John for an "ascetic" lifestyle coheres with his traditional connection with desert areas. On the other hand, Jesus was more of an urban character, comparatively speaking. To locate separately from John would represent a choice on Jesus' part. That choice could very well have represented a different vision about what was central to his mission. Consistent with the change of location was the change of lifestyle.

What would these meals of Jesus have been like? First, the point of the reference is not to say that Jesus was overly fond of food and drink *per se*, but that he was one who could often be found attending banquets. For it is at the banquet that such practices were to be located. Thus the slanderous statement "a glutton and a drunkard" does not picture Jesus as one who ate incessantly but rather pictures him at a festive meal.

The possibility that Jesus spent a lot of time at banquets says a lot in itself. As we have already seen, the banquet as a social institution was a significant event with "liturgical" potential. That is not to say that there was anything unusual or special about Jesus' meals; indeed, they were probably quite normal. But the point is that "normal" meals were still weighty with potential significance.

One such symbolic aspect of meals that Jesus' eating habits would point to is the relation of banqueting to his stance as a sage within the wisdom tradition. By choosing this lifestyle over against that of John, Jesus would be affirming participation in society in a way that John did not. Furthermore, Jewish tradition often pictured the sage at table discoursing about the law (as in Sirach 9:14–15; *Mishnah Abot* 3.3). Similarly, the closest Greek counterpart to the wisdom sage, the Cynic philosopher, was often pictured in the same way.[9] It is quite probable, therefore, that Jesus not only attended banquets, often presumably as simply another guest, but also, in a style consistent with symposium tradition, taught at them as well. This could also correlate with the fact that the sayings of Jesus contain many allusions to the motif of a meal.

The conclusion, then, is that Jesus probably attended banquets and that this was seen to be consistent with his overall message. This is about as much as one can reasonably affirm about the historical Jesus on this question. It does not represent a consensus in scholarship, of course, since such a thing does not exist on an issue like this. The problems connected with historical Jesus research are simply too complex and laden with theological weight for a consensus or even a majority opinion to emerge.

In the final analysis, however, the most important point may be that there is not significant data in the tradition that Jesus founded a specific meal tradition and specified that it be practiced later on. The only such reference we have is in the Pauline version of the Last Supper tradition, "Do this in remembrance of me" (1 Corinthians 11:24, 25). But as we have already noted, this is not even a consistent part of that tradition, since it is missing from the Markan version. Nor does the data about Jesus' preference for banquets represent a model that is commended to his followers. That they interpret it as a model for their time is clear, but in doing so they do not represent themselves as following a command of Jesus. Consequently, what we derive from the historical Jesus data is not the establishment of a specific meal tradition but the possible utilization of ordinary meal tradition as part of a larger teaching process.

2. Meals and the Jesus movement

After the death of Jesus various groups of followers coalesced into groups that we loosely refer to as the Jesus movement. By and large this term refers to groups that formed in the first century in the region around Galilee and Jerusalem. They are especially to be associated with the development of collections of stories about and sayings of Jesus. At this point they tended to exist within the framework of Judaism and initially had very little, if any, sense of estrangement from that tradition. They are to be distinguished from the movement with which Paul was associated, since Paul saw his movement as different from various branches of Jewish Christianity and was not connected with a tradition that relied on stories about and sayings of Jesus for its theology.[10] (The Last Supper text in 1 Corinthians 11:23–26 is an exception to this rule.)

A glimpse into the life of one community of the Jesus movement, the Q community, is provided in the text quoted above (Luke 7:31–35 = Matthew 11:16–10). This text tells a story about Jesus, but obviously does so in a form that is intended to address current needs of the community. It can therefore be read as a reflection of the social situation of the community.

The text envisions a conflict situation in the life of the community, represented by Jesus and John, over against an established religious structure, represented by "this generation." Recent study of the theological content and social context of Q has suggested that phases in the life of the community can be identified by means of a close study of phases in the development of the text.[11] According to this analysis, the community can be seen to move from a relatively stable existence to a period of conflict and finally to a period in which attempts are made to resolve that conflict. The most likely scenario is that it began as a group within the synagogue social structure. At some point, the group became the target of severe criticism from a power group within that social structure, criticism so severe that it eventually led to a painful split with the synagogue.

According to our text, part of the critique has to do with meal practices. That is to say, the critique that is lodged against Jesus in the text is actually representative of a critique that has been lodged against the community. The story about Jesus functions to legitimize their situation. It is as if they are saying to their own community, "No wonder they are criticizing us – they did the same to Jesus and John." Note that whereas the story presents John as an ally in the cause against "this generation," it nevertheless represents a primary identification with the position of Jesus. Jesus is thus functioning as an "authority" to whom they can appeal to legitimize their situation.

The critique, "Behold, a glutton and a drunkard, a friend of tax collectors and sinners," is in essence a charge that one is engaging in sloppy dining habits. It suggests that the Q community has achieved a distinct identity at least partially on the basis of their practicing some kind of separate table fellowship. The fact that they are subject to such a critique at all means that they are still located in the context of the synagogue social structure. But that they are taking meals together separately means that they have already progressed a long way toward the development of a separate identity.

The meals that they eat together are banquets with a festive air. (This is the sense of the phrase "a glutton and a drunkard.") As such, they are interpreted to represent the stance of the wisdom sage vis-à-vis society ("Wisdom is justified by all her children"). This is initially a stance that is positive toward participation in society, but because of the social conflict that has developed, is moving toward a separatist viewpoint (they see themselves as being opposed to "the men of this generation").

Their meals are also characterized as being slanderously open to outsiders. This is the sense of the phrase "Behold . . . a friend of tax collectors and sinners." Both terms in this phrase should be understood as symbolic; they represent scurrilous characters in general. This is clearly the case with the term "sinner," which by no means represents a clearly-defined social category. The same sense may also be applied to the term "tax collector," which would then function as an expletive because it is representative of a particularly hated class of people. The sense of the critique is that this Jesus group was experimenting with the boundaries normal to their social setting.

It is clear that both sides in the conflict take meals very seriously as boundary markers for a community. If this early Christian group can be criticized so harshly for dining with questionable characters, it means that their meals are functioning as significant indicators of community identity. Indeed, since this community originally had its primary social and religious identity in the social setting of the synagogue, its gathering to celebrate a separate communal meal may have been the primary way in which it began to develop a separate community identity. The process whereby this text came to be formed, written down, and preserved is a record of its progress toward an identity as a completely separate community defined at least partially by its communal meals. Indeed, once the synagogue was out of the picture, one may speculate that the social institution of the banquet would have made a significant contribution to the structure of all community meetings from that point on.

Meals in the Gospel communities

None of the Gospels refers to specific practices of their communities. Only Luke addresses this issue, and it is not in the Gospel text but in his second volume, Acts. Therefore, to derive such data from the Gospel texts one must in effect read between the lines. The Gospel narratives certainly present Jesus as a model and reflect tensions and concerns within their communities. The question, however, is how references to meals of Jesus may have functioned to reflect and/or define meal practices in the communities.

1. Mark

The Gospel of Mark is a case in point. Here the Last Supper tradition is given its earliest treatment in a Gospel narrative. What is striking, as has already been pointed out, is that it contains no explicit references to Markan community meals or to a command of Jesus that this be practiced by his followers after his death. Certainly the tradition predates Mark, since it is found in a similar, but not matching, form in Paul. But Mark has used it as part of his narrative just as he does other Jesus traditions.

Recent study has brought to our attention how closely Mark has interwoven this tradition into his overall story. For example, it has been suggested that the idea that the meal is to be associated with an event of "betrayal" rather than an event of "arrest" is to be associated with the narrative purpose of Mark. This is based on the fact that the word translated "betray" is the same term as "deliver up." It contains no inherent reference to betrayal; that idea must be supplied by the context. Therefore when the same term is used in Paul's tradition (1 Corinthians 11:23), it would be better to translate it "deliver up" rather than "betray," contrary to the RSV translation. This is supported by the fact that Paul does not show any awareness of the defection of one of Jesus' followers, since he refers to a resurrection appearance to "the Twelve" (1 Corinthians 15:5).[12]

The idea that one of Jesus' own followers betrayed him can be attributed to a theme in Mark's Gospel in which the disciples are seen throughout to fail to understand Jesus. As the story progresses to a climax, therefore, Judas betrays him (Mark 14:43–45), all the others except Peter flee when he is

arrested (Mark 14:50), and Peter vehemently denies him
(Mark 14:66–72). Special symbolism is given to the Judas
story by the fact that his betrayal is spoken of in the context
of sharing food together (Mark 14:17–21), an action that
normally symbolizes the cementing of bonds of friendship. In the context in Mark, however, Judas is not an
anomaly so much as he is but one more tragic example of
the failure to perceive what discipleship to Jesus really
means.[13]

The meal in Mark has therefore been especially drawn into
the theme of discipleship. This is indicated at several points in
the narrative. For example, at Mark 2:13–17 the tradition that
Jesus was criticized for eating with "tax collectors and
sinners" is made into a story. In this case, however, the
referent has been institutionalized, for the category "tax
collector and sinner" is now interpreted in terms of the
calling of one of the Twelve, who is identified as a tax
collector. Thus the term does not refer to an inclusive
definition of the community meals so much as provide
a legitimization for the current social identity of the
community. That its members identify themselves as equivalent to "outcasts" would then represent their social experience of estrangement from the Jewish community. This
correlates with other references in Mark in which the
disciples are painted as an inner group around Jesus who are
given separate teachings from those provided to the outside
world (as in Mark 4:10–12).

The nature of their estrangement appears to be especially
associated with their meal customs. Mark has included an
extensive debate of Jesus with the Pharisees over purity laws
(Mark 7:1–23). That the followers of Jesus, and likely even
Jesus himself, did not follow the interpretation of the
Pharisees would not in itself represent a departure from the
norms of Judaism. After all, the Pharisees were a minority in
Judaism at this time, and by no means dominated Jewish
society. Yet the harshness and importance of this debate in
Mark suggests that this community was located in an area
where Pharisaic influence was especially strong. Thus this

debate is defined in the text as representative of an estrangement from Judaism as a whole.

What we can derive from these texts is a picture of a
community that is finding itself in conflict with its social
setting. That conflict has especially centered on its meals, so
that the meals constitute a focus for its developing identity as
a sectarian group. What is especially interesting is the way in
which the Last Supper tradition functions in this context. It is
the context in Mark that gives it its specific interpretation.

As has already been mentioned, the Last Supper pericope
in Mark is tied to the overall theme of discipleship, in which
the disciples are seen to fail to live up to its demands. One of
the images that is connected with this theme is that of the
cup. It is woven into the important section in Mark 8–10
where the theme of discipleship is especially developed.[14]
The section begins with Peter's confession, which, in the plot
of Mark, represents the first time that the disciples show any
sign of recognizing the significance of Jesus (8:27–30). This is
followed by three separate programmatic texts in which Jesus
predicts his death, the disciples reject the idea, and a lesson
about discipleship is drawn (8:31–38; 9:30–37; 10:32–45). In
one case, discipleship is described as to "take up his cross and
follow me" (8:34). In another case, it is described in these
terms: "The cup that I drink you will drink; and with the
baptism with which I am baptized, you will be baptized"
(10:39). In both cases, the reference is to the model of the
death of Jesus as the death of a martyr.[15] Thus when Jesus
prays in the garden on the eve of his death, he prays,
"Remove this cup from me" (14:36).

Therefore, when the cup is related to the "blood of the
covenant" at the Last Supper and it is specifically said, "they
all drank of it" (Mark 14:23–24), we are to understand that it
is the cup of martyrdom that they drink. This is the path to
which they have been called and to which they fail to live up
in Mark's story, at least as far as he takes it. It is the path to
which the Markan community is now being called. This
Gospel would therefore be calling for the community at their
community meal to pledge through their sharing in the cup

to follow Jesus even to the point of martyrdom. That that idea is being urged on them so forcefully points up the fact that they must have faced such a severe social crisis that their lives were literally at stake because of the faith they professed (see also 13:9–13). The liturgy at the meal can therefore be seen to represent a ritual response to their specific social situation.

2. Luke–Acts

Luke makes extensive use of meal traditions and literary motifs in his story of Jesus.[16] He uses the meal as a symbol for the ministry of Jesus as a whole. Here Jesus' ministry is seen to be especially directed to outcasts, referred to as tax collectors and sinners (Luke 5:27–32), as well as to the poor, the lame, the blind, and the oppressed, as in the parable of the great banquet (Luke 14:15–24).

The image of the outcast is, however, multivalent in Luke. The tax collector, for example, is absorbed into the larger image of the wealthy person. In some cases, the rich man seems to represent the unrepentant sinner, equated in general with non-believing Israel, as in the parable of the rich man and Lazarus (16:19–31). In other cases, the rich man is called to repentance, and thus is seen to be representative of a figure in the community. This individual is challenged to come to repentance and share his goods with the poor of the community. This theme is represented by a series of texts specific to Luke, including the stories of the rich young ruler (18:18–30), Zacchaeus (19:1–10), and Ananias and Sapphira (Acts 5:1–11).

The image of the sinner, on the other hand, is consistently presented in a positive light. The sinner is seen as the needy one to whom Jesus brings salvation. This process takes place especially at meals, as in Luke 7:36–50. Here Jesus attends a meal at the house of a Pharisee. It is a woman of the streets, a known sinner, whom Jesus allows to wash his feet with her tears and dry them with her hair. This contrasts with the fact that his host did not offer him the customary amenity of a servant to wash his feet. She it is who goes away forgiven.

In many respects the meal imagery in Luke–Acts can be seen to represent the self-identity of the community. This is especially true when the theme of outcasts is defined to include Gentiles as well. Thus the acceptance of Gentiles over Jews at the eschatological banquet functions to legitimize the self-identity of the Lukan community:

> There you will weep and gnash your teeth, when you see Abraham and Isaac and Jacob and all the prophets in the kingdom of God and you yourselves thrust out. And men will come from east and west, and from north and south, and recline [RSV: sit at table] in the kingdom of God (Luke 13:28–29).

The Last Supper text in Luke is found in two forms in the manuscript tradition. In one form, the shorter text, there is a cup-saying with an eschatological theme followed by an abbreviated bread-saying. In the longer text tradition, the bread-saying has been extended and another cup-saying has been added, thus providing a more "traditional" form for this text, and in this case a form that appears to be derived from the Pauline tradition. The long text is an anomaly because it has cup, bread, and cup; the short text is an anomaly because it has cup followed by bread. Neither fits our view of a single line of liturgical tradition; rather, we have here another example of the variety to be found in the data.

We prefer the shorter text as the most likely earliest form, especially since a shorter text, by definition, is usually preferred in text criticism, and in this case it fits better with the literary themes of the Gospel as a whole.[17] Thus here we would have one more example of diversity in the depiction of the Last Supper. Furthermore, we would also have an example of the process whereby uniformity in liturgy was being sought, for the addition of the additional material from the Pauline tradition suggests a later attempt to bring the text into line with a particular liturgical tradition. This attempt, of course, marks a change from the original literary intent of the author.

It is Luke alone of all the Gospel writers who continues his story into the time of the church by writing a second volume, namely, the Acts of the Apostles. Thus we are able to make a more specific connection with meal liturgy by correlating references to communal meals in Acts with the counterparts in Luke's life of Jesus. It is striking that in Acts we have a unique technical term for the community meal: it is called "the breaking of bread" (2:46; 20:7, 11; 27:35). This correlates with the special emphasis given to the breaking of bread in the Jesus story. It is specifically the "breaking of bread" that forms the link between Jesus' Last Supper (22:19b) and the meal of the community (Luke 24:30–31, 35; see also Acts 1:4). The suggestion is that the bread ceremony had taken on a special significance in this community, and, due to the unique nature of the technical terminology in Acts, a significance not widely found in other Christian communities.

What form the bread ceremony took and how it functioned is not entirely clear. In Luke 24:30–35, the sense is that the risen Lord is somehow "known" to them "in the breaking of the bread." But that reference should not be overinterpreted, for in the story it refers to a visionary experience of Jesus, not to a regular community meal. What the story does, therefore, is provide legitimation for the emphasis on the bread in the community meal. When we come across this terminology in Acts, however, in contexts in which community meals are being referred to, the emphasis is not on the presence of Jesus but rather on the process whereby the community is being bonded together (Acts 2:42, 46; 20:7). That imagery best fits the emphasis on the bread, for we can then connect it with common meal tradition as it is also used by Paul, that sharing of food, in this case especially bread, symbolizes the formation of the group into a community (see 1 Corinthians 10:17 and the discussion of Paul below).

The Lukan community, therefore, signified a special form of meal tradition by the terminology "breaking of bread." The Gospel texts play up the theme that the identity of the community as Gentiles who have been accepted fully into the kingdom of God is especially conveyed through the symbolism of the meal. The solidarity of the group centers especially on the bread ceremony as a symbol of community unity and cohesion.

3. Matthew

The other canonical Gospels can be seen to follow similar patterns. Matthew, for example, uses Mark's Last Supper text, but provides a different interpretation because of the different plot within which he places it (see Matthew 26:26–29 in its context). In Matthew the disciples are consistently portrayed as heroes on whose authority the community is built. Thus here, in the Last Supper text, Matthew specifically has Jesus give the bread to the "disciples" and command them both to "eat" and to "drink." The cup-saying from Mark, "this is my blood of the covenant which is poured out for many" (Mark 16:24), becomes "this is my blood of the covenant which is poured out for many for the forgiveness of sins" (Matthew 26:28). Here Matthew has used a different preposition in Greek and added a phrase so that the saying now more clearly reflects Old Testament sacrificial theology.[18]

The effect of these editorial revisions is to give the meal the aura of the archetypal representatives of the community gathered at table with Jesus and receiving a tradition that they will pass on. Furthermore, that tradition has now moved more clearly from general martyrological themes to specific sacrificial themes, laying the groundwork for the later development of the sense of a priest presiding at the altar.

4. John

John exhibits a totally different Last Supper tradition, yet one that, interestingly enough, includes a command to the church to imitate it (John 13:1–15). Thus here there is a reference not to the sharing of food or to the benedictions over the bread and wine but rather to the common act of washing the feet before the meal. This action was normally done by the servant; Jesus gives it symbolic meaning by taking on the garb and role of the servant and washing the feet of his companions himself. Whether this was interpreted liturgically by this community is not clear, but if so, it provides still another example of variation in early Christian liturgy.

Another tradition in John is the famous "sacramental" text at 6:53–54:

> Jesus said to them, "Truly, truly, I say to you, unless you eat the flesh of the Son of man and drink his blood, you have no life in you; he who eats my flesh and drinks my blood has eternal life, and I will raise him up at the last day."

This text has been interpreted as a tradition that was added to John at a later period by a different editor.[19] This is suggested by the fact that it does not fit well in its context, for earlier in John 6 the sense of Jesus as "bread of life" is christological and represents one of the many metaphors in the Gospel for Jesus. Thus the proper response to Jesus as "bread of life," as to him as "water of life," is to respond with a faith that truly "sees" him as divine. To make the switch to a substantive definition of Jesus as bread by means of his flesh that is eaten is an anomaly not only in this context but also in the Gospel as a whole. However, it may represent a stage in the development toward later liturgical themes connected with the "sacramental" interpretation in which bread and wine are given a more substantive identity with the sacrificial flesh and blood of Jesus. At the least, it certainly provides further evidence for the variety of interpretations of the Christian meal to be found in the New Testament texts.

Paul and the banquet at Antioch

As Paul himself was painfully aware, he came on the Christian scene as a latecomer. Certain features of the movement were already in place. Others were still under development. Paul himself actively and energetically contributed to that development. That is to say, while he accepted traditional forms and formulations that were passed on to him, he nevertheless felt few constraints on his impulses to interpret and adapt these as he saw fit. The theological justification for his creative input that he presented time and again was his "calling" by God as "apostle to the Gentiles" (as in Galatians 1:11–17; 1 Corinthians 1:1; Romans 1:1). Under this commission, he went about challenging the movement and calling it to account for its failure to respond adequately to the message of God as contained in his calling.

The first time we come across a meal in a community of Paul is in a conflict situation. It is the famous incident at Antioch, which is given a brief but pointed description in Galatians 2:11–14:

> But when Cephas came to Antioch I opposed him to his face, because he stood condemned. For before certain men came from James, he ate with the Gentiles; but when they came he drew back and separated himself, fearing the circumcision party. And with him the rest of the Jews acted insincerely, so that even Barnabas was carried away by their insincerity. But when I saw that they were not straightforward about the truth of the gospel, I said to Cephas before them all, "If you, though a Jew, live like a Gentile and not like a Jew, how can you compel the Gentiles to live like Jews?"

The text clearly indicates that communal meals were already a regular part of the worship gatherings of the various early Christian communities. This is simply accepted by all concerned; it needs no specific justification. The connection of these meals with "worship" and "liturgy" must be assumed as well. The conflict clearly indicates that these meals were seen as activities carrying considerable theological weight in and of themselves without the need for further interpretation.

The form and interpretation of the Christian meal at Antioch appears to be analogous to that of the banquet of any ancient group or club. The meal is functioning as a boundary marker, defining the special identity of this group. The theme of social bonding is especially strong, since the meal is evidently an important means toward creating a sense of community in the group. It is quite likely as well that further worship activities of the community took place at the table, since it would be such a natural place for such activities.

The conflict developed because a group arrived from the Jerusalem church who would not eat with "the Gentiles" of the Antioch church. They represented a specifically Jewish position within the early Christian movement. It is quite likely, therefore, that they were following some version of the Jewish dietary laws. What should be noted is that both Peter and Paul, as well as Barnabas and other Jewish members of the Antioch church, saw no reason themselves to follow the dietary laws. Yet they do not appear to have defined themselves as reprobates from Judaism.

There was in fact a great deal of variety in first-century Judaism in regard to the dietary laws.[20] It was the Pharisees who had redefined the traditional dietary laws to refer not just to the temple, which was the normal view, but also to the daily table. This view was associated primarily with the Pharisees and, since they were a minority group at this time, was by no means a majority view in Judaism. Consequently, it would not be unusual to find non-Pharisaic Jews who did not apply the dietary laws to their daily lives.

The idea that a Jew could not eat at the table of a Gentile had a different, though related, history. This idea appears to have derived primarily from the restriction against idolatry in biblical tradition. According to this tradition, since all Gentiles were idolators, all Gentile foods were potentially polluted by having been in contact with idols. Thus even wine, a commodity not normally connected with kosher laws, was prohibited if it came from a Gentile source.[21] This variation of the dietary laws appears to have had a form independent of the Pharisaic tradition, since it occurs in such a form, for example, in Acts 15:19–20, where the only restrictions prohibiting Jews from eating with Gentiles are those connected with idolatry. There is no mention here of clean and unclean meats or ritualized handwashing, for example.

In Antioch, however, the form of dietary laws being promoted must have been related to the Pharisaic tradition, since Paul interprets this to be tantamount to "living like a Jew" (Galatians 2:14). Later, however, when he meets up with problems concerning "meat sacrificed to an idol," he does not see it as a major problem; he can take it or leave it (1 Corinthians 8).

Several interpretations of the Christian meal are evidenced in the text from Galatians 2:11–14 quoted above. To the Jewish Christians from Jerusalem, the meal served to define their solidarity with a specific aspect of Jewish tradition. Indeed, to a certain extent the practice of the dietary laws drew boundaries not only between them and the non-Jewish world but also between them and the rest of the Jewish world, just as it did for the Pharisees. This was a sectarian view, then, both within Judaism as a whole and within the early Christian movement. Furthermore, one might speculate that their meal had the aspect of a covenant meal, especially since they were also associated with the espousal of circumcision, the sign of the covenant (Gal. 2:12). If so, the sense would not be that of a "new" covenant, but the traditional Jewish sense of covenant.

Neither Peter nor Paul nor any other of the Hellenistic Jews in their circle at Antioch subscribed to this view. There is no indication that the keeping of some version of the dietary laws had ever been a part of the Judaism they espoused, since they were able to dine freely with Gentiles and yet had not rejected their Jewish heritage. However, Peter apparently routinely accepted the dietary standards of the Jerusalem group whenever he dined with them in Jerusalem, and, just as routinely, accepted the dining customs of the Christians at Antioch when he dined with them.

This routine acceptance of both groups was no longer possible when they met together at Antioch, however, for in this case Peter suddenly had to choose between them, and, by doing so, take on the appearance of rejecting the other group. He and the other Jewish Christians with him chose to dine with the visitors. They apparently saw no major problem with this. One could imagine them going overboard trying to make the visitors feel welcome. Paul, however, saw the issue differently.

To Paul, the issue involved fundamental values of the Christian faith. His interpretation, however, can be seen to be derived from the social code of ancient meals. He saw the communal meal as a highly effective, fundamental means for drawing boundaries and establishing community identity. Consequently, when the Jerusalem group would not dine with the Antioch group, he interpreted this action as a sign of boundaries being drawn *within* the community. Here Paul can be seen to be a strong believer in the power of liturgy. He saw the action of the Jerusalem group as an act of ritual exclusion.

Consequently, for Paul it was not just a matter of customs or of one group insulting another; it was a matter of basic theology. For him, liturgy had to cohere with theology. The theology that all espoused stated that "justification" was through "faith in Jesus Christ" for both Jews and Gentiles (Gal. 3:15–16). The liturgy as they had just practiced it belied that theology. Liturgically, they had proclaimed two gospels, not one. For Paul, then, the primary function of the meal was community formation, and to gather for two meals would mean in effect that there were two communities, not one.

Paul did not necessarily win the day, however, since even Barnabas accepted the view of Peter. Most scholars consider it likely that Paul's split with Barnabas and the Antioch church began from this point (see also Acts 15:39–40). This would mean that the view of Peter represented a specific stance as well, not just an *ad hoc* response. Peter's view is not immediately available to us, but we can speculate about what it might have been.

Like Paul, Peter must have placed the highest value on the place of the meal in community formation. For him, however, the local bonds were prior and sufficient. He did not see the necessity for a universal liturgy into which all variations would be absorbed. One can therefore speculate that, whereas Paul defined the effectiveness of liturgy in terms of its coherence with a larger theological picture, Peter defined it in terms of its coherence with the needs and experiences of individual groups. In this way, Peter's position is not seen as either theologically or liturgically naive, nor is it hypocritical, as Paul would have it. Rather, it is a view that takes an equally strong position on the power of liturgy and an equally strong reliance on the social code of ancient meals, but looks at the social bonding function of the meal from a local rather than global perspective. Consequently Peter's view can be seen as one that sees liturgy as a way to recognize and affirm diversity in the group.

Paul and the "Lord's Supper" at Corinth

In 1 Corinthians 11:17–34, Paul addressed problems of the Christian meal at Corinth. The language of the text suggests that meals were regular parts of their worship services. The parallelism of the phrase "when you assemble as a church" (11:18) with "when you come together to eat" (11:33) suggests that the same event is being referred to. Furthermore, Paul does not seek to justify or explain the meal, but is simply trying to see that it is carried out effectively. The question never arises whether they should have a meal, nor does Paul entertain that idea. Rather, he wants to correct the form their meal has taken. The assumption throughout is that meeting for meals was the norm for early Christian groups.

The first section of the text identifies the problem:

> When you meet together, it is not the Lord's supper that you eat. For in eating, each one goes ahead with his own meal, and one is hungry and another is drunk (11:20–21).

After this Paul quotes the Last Supper tradition (11:23–26), provides his own interpretation of the tradition (11:27–32), and finally proposes a solution: "So then, my brethren, when you come together to eat, wait for one another" (11:33).

In brief, the problem was that some were beginning to eat before others, or were otherwise eating separately, and as a result were getting more food. This brought about the situation that "one is hungry and another is drunk" (11:21). The solution was that they should eat together. The basis for the solution was an interpretation of the Last Supper tradition that centered on the term "body." This term was given a Pauline twist and interpreted as a metaphor for the community, as in 12:12–27. Accordingly, what they were to do was to "discern the body" when they ate and drank (11:29). This they would do when they ate together, for in this way they would exemplify the unity that is to characterize the banquet.[22]

That is a summary of the main argument of the text. Now let us look more closely at the constituent parts of the meal as Paul understood it. First, note that the term "Lord's supper" at 11:20 refers to the banquet as a whole, for it is when they do not eat together that it is profaned. Consequently, the Last Supper tradition can be seen to provide a focus for the interpretation of the meal and perhaps a model for the benedictions over the bread and wine, but it by no means represents the totality of the event. Nor does it function as an authoritative version of the meal, since Paul develops an interpretation of his own that has only a vague relation to the tradition.

How the meal has gone astray has been explained in various ways. It is suggested, for example, that some of the members of the community may have been wealthier than others. They would have had the leisure time to gather early for the meal, while others might still have been at work. The conflict may thus have been caused by differences in social status of the members and the importation of those differences into the community meal, with the attendant expectations that they be given the honor they deserved.[23]

What lies at the root of Paul's interpretation is the common meal tradition. The central meaning of the meal here, as it was in Antioch, is its function in ritualizing social bonding. Here Paul pays careful attention to the ritual process itself. The primary symbol for social bonding is eating together. This is disrupted, as it was in Antioch, if separate groups or "factions" are formed. The act of gathering in the same place at the same time has ritual force.

Social bonding is also signified by the act of sharing food. Paul refers to this concept in 1 Corinthians 10:16: "Because there is one bread, we who are many are one body, for we all partake of the one bread." Here the symbolism is that the sharing of bread together serves to ritualize the bonds that make them into a community or "body." It is a concept that is derived from meal tradition. Plutarch, for example, refers to the same idea in connection with the sharing of wine: "Indeed, just as the wine must be common to all, so too the conversation must be one in which all will share" (*Table Talk* 614E). When Paul utilizes the traditional equation of the bread with "body" (see 11:24) as the center of his specific interpretation, he is apparently referring to the ritual enactment of this meaning in the act of sharng bread.

The same theme of sharing as the primary motif of banquet ethics is found later in 1 Corinthians 14. Here, as in the symposium tradition (see the passage from Plutarch above), the conversation at community gatherings should be conducted in such a way that all can participate (1 Corinthians 14:26–33). Since the setting is related – the discourse takes place "when you come together" (14:26) – and the ethical values are so closely related, it is quite likely that the occasion referred to is the same. That is to say, the discourse described in 1 Corinthians 14 takes place at the same meeting in which the meal is eaten and most likely as their version of the symposium following the meal.

Thus Paul's interpretation throughout can be seen to be drawing on meal tradition. In doing so, he clearly sees it as a powerful form of expression, or "social code," in his culture. Indeed, he gives the meal liturgy such significant weight that he equates the banquet conducted properly with 'proclaiming the Lord's death" (11:26), for it is the liturgy rather than an accompanying spoken text to which this phrase should be seen to refer. The idea is that "the Lord's death" is proclaimed not so much in word but in liturgical witness. It is proclaimed in the act of formation and celebration of the community through the eating of a festive banquet together, a community brought into existence by means of the death of the Lord.

The eucharist in the Didache

While none of the New Testament texts provides a liturgical "script," the Didache provides an example of a text that does. The Didache is a church order document that is thought to have been written in Syria toward the end of the first century CE, but which is likely to contain traditions from earlier periods.[24] It is thus roughly parallel in date and provenance to many of the New Testament documents. Here in chapters 9 and 10 we find our earliest recorded eucharistic prayers. A portion of that text is as follows:

> And concerning the eucharist, hold eucharist thus: First concerning the Cup, "We give thanks to thee, our Father, for the Holy Vine of David thy child, which thou didst make known to us through Jesus thy child; to thee be glory for ever." And concerning the broken Bread: "We give thee thanks, our Father, for the life and knowledge which thou didst make known to us through Jesus thy child. To thee be glory for ever. As this broken bread was scattered upon the mountains, but was brought together and became one, so let thy Church be gathered together from the ends of the earth into thy kingdom, for thine is the glory and the power through Jesus Christ for ever" (Didache 9:1–4).

This eucharist is distinctive in many respects. It should be noted that there is no reference here to a Last Supper tradition, or to the death of Jesus, or to words of Jesus interpreting that death. The meal is not presented as a continuation of something started by Jesus. Nor is it interpreted as a commemoration of Jesus' death. While it does emphasize a special interpretation to be given to the cup and bread, it does not connect them with the death of Jesus but rather with a general sense of community solidarity. It also presents an unusual order in which cup comes before bread, an order found elsewhere only in Luke (and perhaps in 1 Corinthians 10:16).[25]

Thus the eucharist celebrated by this community made no apparent reference to the death of Jesus nor to a last meal tradition. Rather, it emphasized the social bonding of the community through the sharing of wine and bread and connected with it a hope and longing for a joyous eternal destiny with God.

Summary and conclusion

Examination of representative New Testament texts has brought to our attention the variety of forms and interpretations that were given to the Christian meal. Thus we have found that the meals of Jesus, to the extent that they may have taken on any special meaning, are best to be seen as following the model and lifestyle of a sage in the wisdom tradition. It is not likely that such meals placed any strong emphasis on community formation.

It is when we profile the meals of the Jesus movement, as typified in the document Q, that we find the development of a sense of community formation. Here an increasing estrangement from the Jewish community of which they were a part caused them to develop a heightened sense for the way in which a meal defines boundaries. In this case both inclusion and exclusion were given special emphasis as meal ideology was utilized to give cohesion and self-identity to the group as well as to provide ways to legitimate the inclusion of controversial new members.

The tradition of the Last Supper appears in our documents in such varied forms that we must refer to it not as one tradition but as many. Furthermore, these traditions continued to attract new forms and interpretations as they were taken up and adapted to new social situations in the churches. One set of traditions placed the emphasis on formulaic benedictions said by Jesus over the bread and wine. These tended to center on interpretations of the death of Jesus but used different formulas and formations. Furthermore, when these traditions were utilized in the communities represented by our texts they were given still further emphases and interpretations.

In addition to the Last Supper traditions, we have numerous other variations on meal formations, so much so that we cannot account for them as variations on one theme. And by no means can we refer all of them to the Last Supper tradition. Thus there is a general phenomenon in which early Christian communities, like other groups in the ancient world, utilize meals as a central part of their community activities. But also like other groups in the ancient world, they adapted the meal to fit differing needs and emphases.

Thus in both Mark and Matthew we have Last Supper traditions that include eucharistic sayings of Jesus, but in Mark the emphasis is on the cup of martyrdom, while in Matthew an idealization of the heroes of the faith gathered at table seems to predominate. Luke, on the other hand, presents a tradition (in the "short text" version) which tends to transfer the emphasis from the death of Jesus to another theme, the future consummation of the plan of God. Thus the emphasis in Luke's community (as exemplified in Acts) is on the breaking of bread as a symbol for community unity and cohesion without apparent reference to the death of Jesus. Similar themes are found in the Didache, but in a different form. Here we find no references to a last meal of Jesus or to Jesus' death, but rather specified eucharistic prayers in which the emphasis is on celebration of community solidarity and an expression of hope and longing for the joyous reward of the future.

The Last Supper tradition is given still another twist in John 13, where reference is made to the death of Jesus, but connected not with the bread and wine but with the ritual of footwashing, a ritual which is then enjoined as the central liturgical act of the community at its meals. In a separate Johannine tradition, in John 6, the death of Jesus is concerned with the consuming of bread and wine, and in a form which seems to prefigure later sacramental interpretations; here, however, no connection is made with a Last Supper tradition. One is therefore struck not only by the distinctiveness of the meal traditions in the Johannine community but also by the indication that they seemed to have changed over time.

Finally, several distinct meal traditions are evidenced in the Pauline documents, beginning with the reference in Galatians 2 to the Antioch controversy. Here Paul refers to at least three different interpretations of Christian meals, his own and those of James and Peter. The party of James, evidently a Jewish–Christian group, seems to have celebrated a meal which affirmed their identity as Jews and as full participants in the Jewish covenant (hence the emphasis on circumcision). Peter, on the other hand, while evidently acknowledging the importance of the communal meal as constitutive of community identity, seems to have allowed and perhaps even affirmed diversity of interpretation.

Paul provides us with the most extensive and sophisticated interpretation. The meals at his churches, evidently like those of all other early Christian groups, were modeled on the Greco-Roman banquet and provided a ritualization of social bonding. Paul utilized a separate version of a Last Supper tradition, but gave it his own interpretation. According to his interpretation, special emphasis was placed on the power of a meal, when conducted according to proper rules of etiquette (and theology), to break down boundaries and create the kind of community solidarity that should characterize what the church was to be.

What seems to have been held in common in every instance where the communal meal was practiced was a sense of the function of the meal in defining boundaries and bonding a community together, ideas that were derived from common meal tradition. In adapting this tradition, differing communities were responding to specific aspects of their own social situations and were doing so using a ritual "language" that was especially meaningful in their culture. This process can therefore be proposed as primary to the early developments in Christian meal liturgy.

· 4 ·

Celebrating at Many Tables Today

The new picture of the diverse origins of Christian eucharistic practice in the first century that has been proposed in Chapters 2 and 3 promises substantial help in the renewal of worship in our day. Although on the surface the discovery of a variety of early eucharists, rather than just one, seems problematic for worship today, in fact it provides impetus and support for a number of important liturgical developments.

Of course, it does create some problems as well. In this chapter we will first examine the creative eucharistic impulses encouraged by this new picture. Then we will address the difficulties raised for congregations today by the multiple origins of the eucharist in the first century.

There are five creative perspectives that this new picture of the early churches' meals offers congregations in our day. They are:

1. It endorses the current variety of eucharistic practices and undermines various churches' claims to represent the one true eucharist.

2. It invites churches today to compose and revise their Lord's Supper celebrations in creative dialogue with their particular social settings.

3. It provides a rationale and impulse for opening up obtuse and formulaic gestures to creative interplay with the issues of the particular communities and individuals.

4. It places important additional emphasis on the eucharist as an act of a community.

5. It provides a model for respecting differences while expressing connectedness within today's worship settings.

Each of these new perspectives on worship comes directly from the portrait given in the last chapter of the different Christian "eucharists" in the first century. Of course, we are not suggesting that this revision in our understanding of the first century can in itself produce liturgical renewal. We do, however, think that this new understanding lends crucial support to certain efforts at renewal. It also calls into question certain characterizations of liturgical change as untraditional.

The variety of eucharists endorsed, the claims to unique truth undermined

This revised picture of first-century meals is an endorsement of the variety of church practices of the eucharist to be found throughout the churches today. Since the communities of the first century had a range of both practice and interpretation of their sacred meals, a similarly wide range today seems quite acceptable. Our portrait of the differences between the Johannine meals and those in the Pauline circles, for example, makes today's differences between the Roman Catholic mass and the Presbyterian communion seem quite normal.

We live in a church situation where the diversity of understanding and practice of the Christian sacred meal is so great that we do not even have a common term for it. Some call it the "mass," others the "Lord's Supper," some "communion," and yet others the "eucharist." The lack of a common term. is not just a vocabulary problem. It reflects many real differences in the ways the event happens and is interpreted. But, given what has been shown in Chapter 3, there is no need to see these differences as at odds with the way the Christian sacred meal started.

In fact, since there seems to be no actual "original" Lord's Supper model, either in the scriptures themselves (remember, the Last Supper texts themselves are quite contradictory) or in history, the push for unanimity of eucharistic practice seems far less urgent. The first-century churches themselves had different meals and meal interpretations, so why should we expect a singular practice or interpretation in twentieth-century churches? Whatever the claims for a common eucharistic practice within a denomination or for the whole Christian community, they can no longer be made through an appeal to the first century. When interdenominational committees push for common echaristic services or when the Vatican urges all Catholics to say the same mass, their arguments now must stand or fall on their own merits without recourse to a moment of origin in the first century.

Similarly, it should be obvious that the different churches' claims to represent the one true eucharist have even less to recommend them than before. Here also any credibility that such claims might have must now depend on whether those eucharists can demonstrate in themselves some inherent ownership of the truth. Of course, growing awareness of the wide variety of Lord's Supper practices has tended to discredit the churches' assertions that their worship is the one true form. But now such cases are made even more problematic by the fact that there was not one, but a number of early church sources for the eucharist.

Such a new perspective clearly raises questions about the Roman Catholic/Protestant debates on whether the Christian sacred meal is an experience of the presence of Christ or one of memorializing him. For centuries both these communions have been claiming scriptures as their allies in the fight to demonstrate that their particular interpretation of the eucharist was correct.

Now it is clear that neither case can be convincing, because at the very earliest stages there were different meals that tended to emphasize one or the other or neither meaning of the "eucharist." The first-century churches clearly imputed a variety of meanings and carried on a diversity of practice from the very beginnings, and neither the Catholic theology of eucharistic presence nor the Protestant memorial meal can claim to be the original meaning of the Lord's Supper.

Similarly, the diversity of leadership and leadership styles at table in the twentieth century appears to be more a strength than a problem in the light of the first-century data. The fact, for instance, that in some present-day congregations lay people preside over the table, while in others it is a privilege reserved only for the clergy, now need not be seen as a problem. There was great variety not only in first-century meals but also in the forms of leadership as well.

The disputes in today's Christian community about women's leadership at the table are similarly enlightened by the variety of first-century Christian meals. The claim by the Church of England and the Roman Catholic Church that women may not consecrate the elements because that is not the way it happened originally looks very weak in view of the diversity of meals in the early stages of Christianity. It is true that the Revelation to John clearly attacks any involvement of women in leadership and that 1 Corinthians 14:33b–36 commands women not to speak. But in 1 Corinthians 11:2–22 Paul assumes leadership of women at the ritualized meal, since the "prophecy" in which they engage apparently takes place at the meal meetings. There is also much in the Gospel of Luke to suggest that women took this kind of leadership as well in the Lukan milieu.[1]

Most crucial, of course, is the scholarship in Chapter 3 that shows that there were different first-century meals at the beginning, not just one original event with a male figure at its head. There is a real possibility that some early Christian meals did indeed give special and exclusive leadership to men and elected officials in some way during the meal. But it is equally clear that the leadership patterns were so diverse that one cannot claim original authority for any single group within Greco-Roman and Christian meal settings.

Even the current denominational differences in words of consecration at communion now look more like a reflection of the early churches than violations of a universal formula. In the first century, various groups said a variety of prayers at the meal, over the bread, and at the point of the pouring of the cup. The New Testament itself gives three quite different formulations (Paul, Luke, Mark) of the words of institution. The very different traditions reflected in the Didache and the Gospel of John make it clear that the words said at Christian meals in the first century may have been at least as diverse as those being said in the twentieth century.

The diversity of setting and frequency of the eucharist in our day has been a matter of much controversy. The more "liturgical" or "Catholic" churches have emphasized daily and weekly celebrations, while many other Protestants have been debating between monthly and quarterly Lord's Suppers. Similarly, many different local churches and even some dioceses have been caught up in disputes about whether eucharists can be celebrated regularly in homes or in other secular settings.

But in the light of the research outlined in Chapter 3 the differences between those who celebrate the Lord's Supper daily, weekly, monthly, or quarterly are more reflections of the origins of the Christian meal than digressions from it. Close examination of the different first-century traditions shows no clear pattern of frequency or setting. It appears that some of the meals were held irregularly (the early Jesus tradition), some weekly on the Lord's Day (the Johannine tradition), some perhaps daily (Luke) in addition to other rhythms or occasions (Paul).[2] The settings appear to have been mainly in homes, and certainly the practice of a sacred space for the meal had not developed.

Creative composition and revision of the eucharist in dialogue with one's social setting

The portrait of various first-century Christian meals functioning in diverse creative ways relative to the different social circumstances of their communities invites churches today to compose and revise their Lord's Supper celebrations in creative dialogue with their particular social settings. Since there is no one original meal moment to which the churches can appeal, and since the very earliest meals of Jesus and the churches reflect a series of improvizations on a general meal practice in order to address particular social and theological issues, the churches today can create, revise, restore, and reform their eucharists in terms of the needs of their people.

The first-century meals then become an impetus not for the wide variety of churches in the world today to agree on one practice, but for each of the churches to engage in a process of creative application to their particular tradition and social circumstances. This means that a lively eucharist both in the first and twentieth centuries depends on an ongoing reflection on and interaction with the social circumstances of the particular community. Churches with different social dynamics can be encouraged to celebrate their sacred meal according to what best addresses their situation. We have already seen how this occurred in the first century. Let us now take a look at how it occurs in the twentieth century. Three examples will suffice to show a breadth of application.[3]

1. A congregation in transition
Johnson Memorial Baptist Church was a mostly elderly congregation in a community which was experiencing many new younger adults – both with and without families – moving into the area. Some of the new residents had begun coming to church, although many who visited did not come back again. A few did stay and had made it their new church home.

It wasn't that the older people weren't friendly or open. They were actually quite eager to make adjustments, and most were even ready to hand over the reins to younger leaders.

The communion service, which was held every six weeks, was a heavily coded, stylized, and silent event. It was a very important part of the elderly congregation's life. There were women who had had the jobs of cutting up the little cubes of bread and of laying the altar cloths for forty years. Each of the ushers and elders who helped pass out the grape juice and bread in the pews had their special aisles from which they had been serving for at least a generation.

The pastors, upon their arrival, always had to learn a series of signals and a rhythm for the communion service. It was made clear that several of the widows needed several minutes to pray silently after communion. And, although no one ever announced it, the congregation always stood up after communion and sang "Blessed Be the Tie That Binds Our Hearts in Christian Love."

This communion service in the last twenty years had become a way of stabilizing a changing world for the congregation. Many of their children, whom they had hoped would stay in the community, had moved away. The many larger societal changes around the older generation had made them feel spiritually embattled. The communion service, however, confirmed the reality of the life they had lived. It celebrated the commitments they had made to each other and the accomplishments they had achieved. It was a caring, stable event in what often seemed like a crazy and cruel world.

When a new pastor came, she and several of the newer members decided to make some changes in the communion service. They kept those who cut the bread, laid the cloths, and distributed the elements. But in each case they asked several others to join the older work group.

More drastic was the change in mood. Instead of mostly silence or organ playing, there was much more speaking and exchange. They introduced the passing of the peace as a part of the communion service. When the pastor stood before the table, she asked for (and because she had orchestrated this ahead of time, she received) spoken sentence prayers of thanksgiving and petition. At the end, she asked the congregation to choose a favorite hymn to sing. Sometimes this was "Blessed Be the Tie ..." But sometimes it was another hymn or even a song that wasn't in the hymnal.

The net effect was that there was much more communication between people. The communion itself became a place where some of the newer and older people could get to know one another. Instead of expressing the strong communion of the generation that had been together for so long, the service began to build another communion between the older and the newer. This, of course, also communicated to other visitors a spirit of openness and flexibility. A revision of eucharistic practice toward informality enabled the personal interaction necessary for the integration of new people and communicated to them the possibility of their becoming accepted and influential parts of the congregation.

2. The congregation in the middle of social upheaval

In the St Mark's parish area chaos, crime, and social disorder dominated daily life. There were constant muggings and break-ins, even into the church itself. With tax revenues declining sharply, the municipal government seemed in trouble, and certainly not interested in St Mark's area of the city.

The relatively small and diverse congregation was distressed about the developments in the neighborhood, and had some programs that acted as a haven for many in the area. A tutoring program for elementary children had also become a place for them to go after school, since most of them were latch-key children. There was also a counseling office for battered women in the church building.

The eucharist at St Mark's was highly structured and formal. The priest was always fully vested. There was always a procession. No matter how many people came on Sunday morning or whether or not there were disruptions, the candles, the paraments, the three scripture lessons, the collects for the day, the acolytes, and the bishop's chair were always in place.

The congregation drew great support from this eucharist, and the occasional new people who joined remarked on how important this eucharistic style had been for them in deciding to stay. This structured and predictable eucharistic practice provided stability and reassurance.

In such a setting, a formal eucharist with set movements, vestments, and words functioned to image social order for a traumatized population. This Lord's Supper was not impersonal. It was done with genuine personal presence and particular address in prayer and sermon to personal and social issues. But the stability of practice in itself ministered to the people whose lives were so often disrupted by social disorder. The formal eucharist served as an image of a stability and order which their world could have, but didn't.

3. The diverse congregation

There were several distinct and different groupings of people at Emmaus United Church of Christ. A core of five extended families made up a fairly tight-knit grouping of fifty or so people. The nearby college population also contributed about thirty to forty students and three to six professors to the membership and constituency. And, finally, in the past decade a number of Asian families had begun to attend.

Members of these distinct groups were each quite established entities of the congregation, but the individuals from each grouping tended to have very little to do with those from another. There did not seem to be any blatant bigotry, simply a tendency for each group to stay in its own sometimes narrow company.

The worship committee decided to make use of a longstanding tradition of pot-luck suppers for some liturgical experimentation. They held a series of eight pot-luck suppers on the first Sunday evening of the month. They set up tables for eight persons around the fellowship hall. Of course, those who came tended to sit at tables where those from their own grouping were.

To begin the evening everyone sang a hymn together. Then the chairperson of the worship committee asked each table to come up with its favorite hymn or dessert or movie as a group (there was a different assignment each month). Each table spent five minutes discussing the question, and then reported to the whole assembly. With everyone ready to eat, the leader then said a brief blessing over the food.

She then asked everyone to come up and serve themselves with food and told them to pick up a number at the end of the table, which would designate a new table at which they were asked to sit for the rest of the meal. Since these numbers were distributed randomly, the result was that the reshuffled tables were very mixed in terms of their composition.

Conversation at the tables was a bit slower when people sat down at their new places, but by the end of the main course the chatter level was almost back to the same level. At the end of the meal, the worship chairperson asked each table to prepare for a time of prayer by identifying one thing for which they were thankful and one person or group for whom they wished to pray.

The groups took a few moments to discuss this. Then the leader led the congregation in prayer. She asked that after each petition or thanksgiving the congregation respond by saying "Hear us, O God." She also welcomed people to add other sentence prayers that an individual might feel called to add, and some did just that.

In this situation where socio-economic conditions were relatively stable, but where the membership was diverse in its class, racial, family type and age groupings, such a "Lord's Supper" at a pot-luck supper helped the congregation work on the differences. Such a meal allowed for recognition of the differences. Particular groups did need to sit together at tables, in order to keep their particular identity within the larger congregational mix. On the other hand, the informal pot-luck setting also allowed for some of the boundaries between class, age, family type, and race to be provisionally crossed so that new personal connections necessary for both personal growth and congregational coherence occurred.

We could give many other examples of how the particular way in which a congregation celebrates its sacred meal reflects and nourishes the social reality of the local church. But from the above three examples it is clear that the twentieth century has a potential for creative composition and revision of the Lord's Supper in dialogue with social settings that is similar to the first-century dynamics.

Formula opened up and contemporary concerns integrated

The mix of social interaction and ritual in the first-century meals directs the contemporary churches toward formats in which contemporary social and personal concerns can both shape and be integrated into worship. It provides a rationale and impulse for opening up obtuse and formulaic gestures to creative interplay with the issues of the particular communities and individuals.

Current church practice has implied that the words said and gestures done around the table have been determined by Jesus at the original Last Supper. Therefore, even though they have varied from denomination to denomination, the attitude within local churches about these has been that they were immutable.

No matter on what level one examines the situation, it becomes obvious that the first-century flux was so great that these formulae cannot come directly from an original Last Supper. Not only do we have the great variety of early tradition discussed in Chapter 3; the New Testament renderings of the Last Supper are in conflict with one another. As we have already mentioned, the words of consecration are different in Luke, 1 Corinthians, and Mark. In addition, they all three disagree on when the words were said during the meal.

Of course, a more obvious challenge to the assumption that there is only one true set of words and gestures at the Christian table is the difference mentioned above between the many existing churches today. But given the data in this book, it is now clear that these differences go as far back as the Christian meals themselves.

This means that today's Christians can be encouraged to speak words and make gestures at the eucharistic table that connect the elements of the meal with the elements of people's lives. As the bread and cup are consecrated, it can be both appropriate and enriching to hold up events in the congregation or the world about which the church needs to be thankful or concerned.

Prayers for the sick or the deceased, petitions for the

hungry and the lonely and thanksgivings for family, job, or social accomplishments can all happen at the congregation's table. The table itself need not just contain the elements, but can hold pictures, books, rocks, plants, and memorabilia that are appropriate to the particular moment in the congregation's life. The celebrant can invite persons to join her/him for the prayers and consecration, especially when those persons have special significance or need at that time.

The eucharist emphasized as community act

The clear social contexts for the first-century Christian meals place important additional emphasis on current Christian eucharist being an act of a community. The lack of evidence for individualistic interpretation of the Lord's Supper in the first century challenges much individualistic piety of today and suggests a more collective model.

It is obvious from the descriptions in Chapters 2 and 3 that all the early eucharists were variations on the Greco-Roman banquets. These were events in which people experienced themselves as a group. Their coming together identified their community bonds and boundaries. And within the meal they enjoyed one another, fought with one another, and connected with one another.

This stands in some contrast to the character of many eucharists today in which the churchgoer primarily experiences him/herself as alone before God. There are certain strong strains of both Protestant and Roman Catholic interpretation which have emphasized the individual before God at the table.

This emphasis on the individual at table, rather than the group together at a meal, corresponds in an unhappy way with many isolationist and individualist tendencies within Western cultures. Rugged individualism, especially within American society, has contributed in major ways to the exploitation of the poor, significant damage to the environment, and our inability to live together in families and communities.

Inasmuch as communion can live up to its name and first-century heritage by giving expression to the group life of congregations, it can also minister to our society's desperate need for people to learn to live together.

Differences respected, connectedness expressed

There are two major ways that the New Testament communities modelled the respect of difference while expressing connectedness between people. First of all, the early Christian eucharists seemed to have made very similar distinctions between people to those made in other banquets. By and large it appears that the ranking of guests which occurred in general in Greco-Roman meals was also the practice at Christian meals. Paul makes several references to this, and it is assumed in many synoptic passages. Similarly, distinctions between Jew and Gentile, man and woman, servant and master, rich and poor seem to have been observed in some of the Christian meals.

At the same time, the differences between the way the various Christian groups celebrated and interpreted the meal as outlined in Chapter 2 are a model for the way in which churches today can also have different eucharistic practices.

Both the differences within the particular communities and those between different groups were observed along with the affirmation of a strong connectedness both between the people and the various churches. As we noted in Chapter 2, Greco-Roman meals did this well in any case. They acknowledged the differences between the meal participants through the seating, ranking, and the appointing of meal leaders, while they also at the same time affirmed the bonds between everyone by virtue of shared food, entertainment, and talk.

Similarly, it is clear that first-century inter-church events like the Council at Jerusalem did not want to propose a uniformity of meal practice throughout the churches. They left leeway for differences of meal ceremonies and participation, while affirming the bonds between the churches with some gestures in common.

The ways that first-century meals recognized differences without requiring conformity stand in stark contrast to most worship models today. Both within local churches and larger denominations our major tendency is toward uniformity of eucharistic practice and membership. Most churches represent only one ethnic group. Almost all denominations prescribe exact formulae for what is to be done and said at table.

This flight from difference and imposition of uniformity occurs despite a growing pluralism of population within the larger church, society, and the world. Our situations in general need ways of acknowledging differences while affirming connections. The last three decades of struggle by minorities and women have pointed out that equality is not achieved by attempting to make everyone the same. Both majority rule in democracy and hierarchical rule in some churches enforce sameness.

The need to respect differences while expressing connectedness today can be informed both by the way first-century meals marked differences and the way different New Testament communities improvised within the meal pattern to construct their own particular pattern. Churches in our time can use their own meal rituals as ways of acknowledging difference while expressing connectedness. The case of the Emmaus United Church of Christ discussed earlier in this chapter serves as an appropriate example of how a meal can nourish both difference and connectedness within a community.

The problems for churches today raised by multiple eucharistic origins

Of course, this new vision of many eucharistic variations in the first century does not only bring creative possibilities for worship to the churches. It also brings problems.

The various denominations' appeals to the first century and the New Testament for validation of their particular eucharistic practice as the only and/or true representation of Christian eucharist are undermined. If the first century and

New Testament scriptures actually reflect a diverse application of a general set of meal customs, then any claim today by
a church that it represents the correct and original understanding of the Lord's Supper becomes suspect. We have seen
that such a challenge offers new opportunities. But it is also
necessary to note that it presents church people who have
thought that they were practicing the one true sacred meal
with problems.

Similarly, any church's understanding of its eucharist as
rooted in a real command at a historical Last Supper is
problematic. If the Last Supper texts are products of early
church practice and/or theology, contemporary Christian
self-understanding of the Lord's Supper as repetition of Jesus'
last meal conflicts with the evolving historical picture of the
origins of Christian meals.

A third problem is that the portrait of less formally
liturgical first-century Christian meals relativizes the various
rigid eucharistic practices of contemporary churches. The
various integrations of rituals and social interaction in the
first-century meals pointedly raises issues about the highly
formalized structures of most contemporary Lord's Supper
liturgies. Do not the flexible and informal exchanges of the
Greco-Roman banquet call the highly choreographed and
exactly written character of most eucharists today into
question?

The challenges this approach poses both for churches'
claims to absolute authority and for their need for rigid
liturgical structures have not disappeared in this discussion.
This approach will not be received well by some who need
such absolute authority and such tight structures. In fact, as
suggested above, such needs also have their own social roots
and validity, and may well be addressed by a particular kind
of eucharist for a particular set of people.

It is important, however, to see that the churches today are
experiencing the claim to absolute authority and rigid
structures as a general issue in congregational and denominational life. It is not just in worship practice that the churches
are in conflict about some (mostly powerful and entrenched)

insistence on absolute authority and rigid structures. In the areas of church finances, sex roles, clergy-lay relationships, educational programming, social outreach, and biblical interpretation the issues of absolute authority and rigid structures are central and controversial.

It is crucial, then, to see that some objections to a multivalent eucharist are part of larger value-conflicts that contemporary churches encounter. Although some churches may want to use a highly structured eucharist to address certain specific situations (cf. our example of St Mark's Church earlier in this chapter), the general rigidity and authoritarianism of many approaches to the Lord's Supper today need to be addressed as symptomatic of a general problem in the church communities.

We suggest, then, that the solution to the conflict between the flexible and variable New Testament meals and the highly structured and immutable forms of today's eucharists lies in a much more general answer from the churches to the impulses to become rigid. Today's churches are buffeted by so many changes in society that they seek stability through authoritarianism and traditionalism.

Having lost touch with much of vital and open-ended spiritual dynamism, the churches in many areas have tended to react to the many changes around them with appeals to hierarchical and nostalgic behavior. By and large such authoritarianism and rigidity results in churches losing their ability to adapt to new situations. Often this means that the churches also lose membership, because they cannot adapt to newer populations around them.

The major issue, then, is not the loss of one origin for the Christian sacred meal. It is the larger question of the many threats to the churches, and whether the churches can develop an internal response instead of an authoritarian or formalistic response.

The problem posed by the lack of historical support for the Last Supper's unique authority in church practice seems less formidable. There seem to be two issues with two fairly clear solutions.

Inasmuch as church persons wonder whether it is still legitimate to celebrate the Lord's Supper with the citation of some words of institution, two observations need to be made:

1. There are different words of institution in the various biblical passages concerning the Last Supper. 1 Corinthians, Luke, and Mark disagree in their accounts of what they have Jesus saying and doing. So there is no one set of words the churches have ever been able to call on. Any appeal, therefore, to what Jesus said is on shaky grounds even within the Bible.

2. It is possible for the Lord to instruct the churches beyond the Bible. Just because the words of institution cannot be identified specifically or given historical validity does not mean that the Lord did/does not instruct the churches in this and other ages on how to institutionalize their meals. That is, there is a theological rationale for understanding the Lord to have instructed the particular denominational committees or inspired individuals that determined the words of institution for their particular communion. This, of course, is a much more Catholic notion of both church authority and the teaching of Christ.

The significance of the early church meal diversity in relationship to the contemporary ecumenical movement toward a common eucharist

To apply the diversity of first-century Christian meal practices to the celebration of the eucharist in our day in these ways contrasts strongly with major liturgical reform and research of the past two generations. For the past thirty to sixty years liturgical reform and research has worked for a more unified (and Catholic) practice and understanding of the eucharist.

These efforts have resulted in almost all of the major Protestant eucharistic liturgies moving toward what was articulated as the sacramental understanding and practice of the "early church." Especially the Lutheran and Anglican churches have moved strongly to reassert a eucharist which contains almost all of the elements and interpretations of the Roman Catholic mass. But the United Methodists, the United Church of Christ, the Disciples of Christ, and the Presbyterians have also moved in this direction. Even the most free church denominations like the Baptists, Mennonites, and the Church of the Brethren have at least begun to have communion more frequently.

This movement has produced many helpful results, especially in bringing Protestants and Catholics together where relatively petty doctrinal disputes had previously separated them. It has produced both a sense of a broader Christianity in the various churches and actual agreements on the interpretation of the Lord's Supper between Roman Catholics and major Protestant denominations.

Our proposals do not mean to challenge the value of these movements. Our research does challenge directly their roots within the first century. There is clearly great value in the various Christian movements acknowledging their common heritage (rather than endlessly debating one another on doctrinal differences). But given what we have outlined in Chapter 3 it is no longer accurate to hark back to one unifying early Christian eucharist.

Church leaders who advocate a common eucharist for all denominations and churches used to be able to appeal to both a historical and original Last Supper and a common eucharistic ritual in the "early church." Now neither of these appeals can be made with integrity, as we have shown in Chapter 3. If there is a value to all or many different churches practicing the same eucharist, that value must be explained in terms of our situation today without appeal to a single-moment eucharistic origin.

We would suggest the following ways of integrating our work into these liturgical movements which have unified many denominations around a common eucharistic liturgy in our century:

1. We should state clearly that gathering together Christians who have long been divided by petty doctrinal disputes around a common table practice is in and of itself very helpful

to churchgoers, at least in America. In our country there are so many forces that tend to divide people from one another. That Lutherans, Methodists, Roman Catholics, and Presbyterians are now often doing eucharist in very similar ways has a particular social value.

2. We should correct the liturgical and ecumenical movement's appeal to the first-century churches for support in its effort to unify feuding Christians. No one's case will be served in the long run by a misrepresentation of history.

3. We should question the ability of unified liturgical practice to express the nature of the church and the gospel in the globalized situation of today. In the broad scope of the global church today and even within many congregations where great diversity exists, emphasis on one standard and immutable eucharist is bound to do injustice to some particular groups. Surely the gospel and the church are not to alienate peoples and individuals from the particular strengths of their culture or social situation. It seems difficult to imagine that a God of the good news of love and justice would want a central sacred meal that forced Africans or Asians all to act like Europeans. Even if there are moments for expression of unity through a common eucharistic practice, to generalize such a service and to make it the single kind of Lord's Supper violates the integrity of many cultures and social situations.

What we have noted in Chapters 2 and 3 is that the first century actually gives us a model of several different Christian sacred meals and interpretations. Liturgical unity did not exist in the first century.

4. We should encourage even within movements that strive toward some commonality of eucharistic practice the impulse to adapt and improvize according to the particular needs of the local worshipping body. This has been the main thrust of this chapter. We have suggested that we may learn from the first-century meals how to adapt eucharistic celebrations to different specific congregational settings. Such improvization and flexibility within the eucharistic tradition can revitalize worship itself in our time.

· 5 ·

Eucharistic Theory: Imaging Eternal Truth or Nurturing Social Reality?

After Roman Catholic missionaries had made their first converts in New Guinea, they discovered that the eucharistic sentence, "Behold the Lamb of God," made no sense to the people, since there were no sheep on the island. Noticing that the primary domesticated animals of the island were swine, the priests then began saying mass with the phrase, "Behold the pig of God."

Every fifteen minutes the MacDonalds fast-food chain hosts over 2,000 people for a meal. About forty-five per cent of them are Christians.

In a suburb of St Louis, Missouri, mostly middle-aged, upper-middle income United Presbyterians gather on the first Sunday of the month to hear their pastor preach a sermon and to join him in remembering Jesus' last meal as they eat a small square of white bread and drink a small shot glass of grape juice.

When Peter and his community met for banquets in the first century, they blessed the bread, ate a meal, blessed a cup of wine, and spent the rest of the evening drinking, discussing, and singing. There were rarely any non-Jews present at these banquets, and if there were, they sat separate from the rest of the people at the banquet.

The youth group leader in Oregon led the youth group and the Sunday congregation in the consecration of a bottle of coke and a dozen doughnuts, and then distributed them to the worshippers.

In Cameroun the villagers gather for a feast celebrating the end of the rainy season. They give thanks to Allah for all goodness.

Which of these events is a celebration of a eucharist? Which is not? What makes a eucharist?

It is almost certain that we could find persons of authority who would judge each of the above examples as not meeting their criteria for the Christian sacred meal. On the other hand it is also quite probable we could find persons of authority who would qualify each of the examples as eucharists or Lord's Suppers.

In the history of Christian worship the criteria of correct practice, correct doctrine, and correct spirit have played a significant role in judging what is and is not a Christian sacred meal. None of these criteria have ever worked in anything larger than a sectarian setting. Eucharistic practice has always been so diverse that those who require certain gestures, words, or settings have only been able to justify *their own* practice as the correct one, and have failed to come up with coherent and mutually acceptable standards for groups unlike themselves. Eucharistic theology as a criterion for the event itself has been similarly mired in narrow perspectives, at best coming up with endorsements of its own situation and quick judgment of communities different from its own. And, of course, spirit has remained an intangible and unjudgeable criterion for all but the initiated. Whether people have the right attitude or whether the correct emotions are expressed are questions which cannot be answered objectively.

As Christians and others have had to come to terms with an increasing awareness of a very wide spectrum of sacred meal practice around the world, the question of what constitutes the Christian sacred meal has become complex.

Furthermore, the data about the diversity of early

Christian meals that we have found in this book can serve to complement and extend our contemporary awareness of the wide diversity of scenarios, meanings, and practices related to Christian meal practice. In some ways, it is not just another addition to our awareness of this broad spectrum, but the final example. Now we can no longer attempt to return to the original and unifying meaning, scenario, and practice of the early Christian meal. Rather, we must now deal with an almost bewildering collection of sacred meals into which Christians are invited.

In face of the questionable success of the theologians' and ecclesiastics' criteria of doctrine, practice, and spirit, twentieth-century thinkers have energetically undertaken to fit the eucharist into a larger study of ritual.

For over one hundred years scholars have been looking at rituals around the world and comparing them to the eucharist. This effort – not possible before because there was little knowledge of ritual practices other than our own – has sought to understand human ritual in general. Striking parallels and comparisons between non-Christian rituals and the eucharist have been found. An abundance of new data about ritual from around the world has enabled scholars in religious studies, history, anthropology, and sociology to make some clear proposals about the nature and functions of ritual.

These proposals seem relevant to a clear understanding of the eucharist. Especially in a time when Christians themselves are confused and disoriented by new awareness of so many different non-Christian beliefs and practices, the results of these studies seem important for today's churches to contemplate. Our own demonstration that first-century Christian meals can no longer be asserted to have had a singular and clear meaning also calls for us to consult those scholars in ritual theory who have been addressing the similarities in and diversities of ritual.

Curiously enough, most research in ritual in the past century has not penetrated the churches at all. The academic world, and to a certain extent the art world, has engaged in this examination of the meaning of ritual. But the churches have by and large remained uninformed.

We turn now to a sampling of this thought in the hope of being able to integrate ritual theory with both the biblical data and the theological tasks at hand. Because this ritual theory from the fields of social science and the churches' understanding of their liturgy have not been integrated with one another, our effort here will need to remain basic, and to leave a number of questions unanswered. It is hoped that this attempt will begin a process analogous to the integration of psychological theory into pastoral counseling and socio-logical theory into church social projects over the past thirty years.

Ritual as access to the eternal sacred

The discussion of the meaning of ritual has been dominated in the twentieth century by a series of theorists who have sought to identify several types of ritual action which they find throughout the world and throughout history. Each of these types of ritual action then has a universal meaning that one can find expressed in every society, although perhaps with adaptations to the particular culture. These universal meanings are sometimes social and sometimes more meta-physical, but they apply to humanity as a whole.

The work of the phenomenologist Gerhard van der Leeuw and the anthropologist Arnold van Gennep in the early part of the twentieth century typify some of the first clear efforts to formulate the existence of universal ritual actions.

Van Gennep, for example, classified a certain set of rituals relating to childbirth, adolescence, marriage, funerals, and similar occasions as "rites of passage." He concluded that throughout the world "an individual is placed in various sections of society . . . (and that) in order to pass from one category to another and to join individuals in other sections, he (sic) must submit, from the day of his birth to that of his death, to ceremonies whose forms often vary but whose function is similar."[1] In van Gennep's view, these rituals had universal significance in their ability to relate individuals to their society. His work then became a paradigm for under-standing the universal meaning of ritual itself.

Gerhard van der Leeuw catalogued whole series of parallels of ritual actions in a manner like that of van Gennep but with a much wider sweep.[2] He found the same kind of purifica-tions, sacrifices, sacramentals, divinations, festivals, sacred words, words of consecration, myths, praises, and lallations in different settings.

Mircea Eliade followed these earlier theorists, and used the term "the sacred"[3] to characterize the universal nature of ritual. Eliade suggested that the sacred consisted of two components, "sacred time" and "sacred space," and that the experience of both of these was universal and necessary.[4] Eliade has become the chief representative of this "school" of thought.

Stressing these key concepts of "sacred space" and "sacred time," he led the way in establishing a broad system of categorizing kinds of universal ritual action and analysing their main components.

A primary implication of this universal nature of ritual for Eliade has been that all ritual allows a "communication with"[5] a transcendent reality. "The sacred is saturated with being," he says.[6] Ritual therefore provides access to the sacred and its transcendent orienting perspective.

In particular, Eliade has found examples in which rituals give the world a sense of order for those who participate in them.[7] For Eliade, much ritual is "making the world sacred"[8] and "undertaking the creation of the world one chooses to inhabit."[9]

Eliade and his colleagues have been responding to the growing awareness of non-Western religious expression. They have attempted to understand the many different ritual expressions from non-Western cultures. They have made a strong effort to understand non-Western and Western rituals within a common framework. This has pointed them away from explaining everything in Christian theological terms, since that in itself could be a violation of the terms of the non-Western rituals. But in giving up the Christian theological terms, Eliade has not given up the proposal that all these rituals – Western and non-Western – provide a kind of divine and orienting experience.

The works of the historian Joseph Campbell and the psychologist C. G. Jung have complemented, expanded, and popularized this basic notion that one can categorize ritual actions, and that these types of ritual actions have universal significance. Jung found "archetypes" in the human psyche that he said were universal, and that often corresponded to the universal significance of the types of ritual action proposed by the school of the eternal sacred. So, for instance, the archetypal meaning of decorating a Christmas tree or an Easter egg is far more universal than its Christian context, and is comparable to rites of rebirth the world over.[10] Jung even undertook an analysis of the Roman Catholic mass, in which he showed how each stage and action of the mass corresponded to what he believed to be universal structures of the human psyche itself.[11]

Joseph Campbell compiled the most ambitious global catalogue of ritual (and mythic) actions in his four-volume *Masks of God*, and developed more accessible categories for the types of ritual actions and the nature of their universal meaning. Campbell's *Hero With a Thousand Faces* outlines perhaps the most popular of these categories, and details the stories and rituals throughout cultures and history that celebrate the human ability to transcend and conquer an environment. Before his death Campbell did a twelve-part television series with Bill Moyers on the universal meanings of myth and ritual.

The overall result of the work of van Gennep, van der Leeuw, Eliade, Jung, Campbell, and their followers has been to propose that ritual actions can be arranged into universal types and that the meaning of these types of action can then be generalized. By extension the sacred meal is a universal ritual action and has a generalized meaning.

Van der Leeuw summarizes the implication of this perspective for our understanding of the sacred meal: "Thus every communal meal is not merely a sacrifice but a sacrament

also and, while not being officially recognized as such, a
sacramental. The consecration of food on Easter morning
takes account of these conditions even today: baskets filled
with eggs, bread, salt, ham, and little lambs made of sugar,
are brought to church to be blessed ... On the island of Buru
in the Moluccas, for instance, each clan holds a communal
rice meal, to which each member contributes some fresh rice,
and this is called 'eating the soul of the rice.'"[12]

This school of thought which has dominated ritual theory
for most of the past century has shown how the eucharist fits
into a larger global pattern of ritual actions that make the
world sacred. The eucharist, understood from and integrated
into this global theory of ritual, evokes the sacred and gives
access to the transcendent.

This has applied the generalized meaning of the universal
sacred meal to the Christian eucharist. In this theory the
eucharist then maintains its privilege as providing access to
the holy, but does so as a part of a general category of ritual
meals. It is then not the "Christian" content but the universal
form of the action that makes the Christian meal "sacred."

These theories of ritual do place the eucharist in a somewhat different perspective. To a certain extent they relativize
its importance in that they say it provides access to the sacred
in the same way similar rituals of other faiths do. So from
this point of view it is no longer possible to assert that the
eucharist is unique in its ability to call us into God's presence.
But at the same time these theories integrate the eucharist
into a larger understanding of the sacred. The eucharist is
seen as a type of sacred action. Its special function for the
community remains, but the claim that no other ritual can do
this is gone.

Such a move is of some help in the integration of the
diversity of the early Christian eucharistic events. In the
Eliadean perspective, rituals from other religions which have
similar functions to the eucharist do not detract from the
value of the eucharist. Similarly, a multiplicity of eucharistic
types in the first century need not take anything away from
the value of each different kind of first-century eucharist.

Of course, another benefit of this theoretical perspective is that by integrating the eucharist into a larger ritual perspective, it offers Christianity some help in its struggle against its own chauvinism. Eliade, Jung, and others preserve meaning for the Christian rite while allowing other religious traditions to have a similar meaning.

Interestingly enough, the most recent generation of ritual theorists has not criticized the Eliadean perspective for not being Christian enough, but for still having some implicit Christian chauvinism that impedes their ability to understand ritual in general and the eucharist in particular.

Ritual as nurturing social realities

In the last forty years there have been several serious challenges to this reigning notion of ritual as universal experience of the sacred. These challenges have been grounded in two significant developments: 1. the acquisition of a great deal more data, mainly from the field research of cultural anthropologists and their reports of life and ritual in many different, mainly non-Western settings; and 2. the rekindling of interest in the sociology of religion. Much attention has been given to the re-reading of the nineteenth-century sociologist of religion Emile Durkheim, as theorists have attempted to explain the relationship between rituals and their social settings, especially as described in the new reports of the anthropologists.

In the 1950s and 1960s the French anthropologist Claude Lévi-Strauss made a series of proposals that challenged the notion of the sacred in ritual by asking Durkheimian questions of the new anthropological data. Lévi-Strauss' proposals, which came to be known as structuralism, also challenged to a more limited extent the idea that ritual has universal meaning.[13] Because his work then influenced the next generation of ritual theorists and because his system is extremely complex, we will not examine his thought in any more detail here, but will proceed to the next generation.

Historians of religion and anthropologists, using Durkheim and Lévi-Strauss with more field-study data, have been able to see more clearly the social significance of ritual for the groups involved. These new theories have tended to raise the question whether a theological bias has informed the van der Leeuw/Eliade/Jung/Campbell axis with its proposal for universal meaning and communication with the sacred. The notion that certain human ritual actions throughout the world and history can be given the same meaning sounds suspiciously like Western monotheism. The newer theorists have been reinforced in this challenge by their ability to detail patterns of particular social meaning of different ritual actions for specific groups of people.

Although not entirely abandoning the relationship between ritual and the sacred, the anthropologist Victor Turner's work has emphasized two other dimensions of ritual.[14]

Turner has underlined the importance of ritual in relationship to what he calls *communitas*. This term points to the way in which many ritual actions act to reveal a basic communal structure and to nourish social units of the people who participate in the ritual. Particular rituals seem to be done primarily in order to address particular questions of order, governance, health, and membership in groups. Many of Turner's examples are taken from the Ndembu, an African tribe which he himself studied in the field at several points in his life. Their divination rituals, for instance, have the primary results of governing residence in the village and of healing social rifts. Hence, much more for Turner than for Eliade, the significance of ritual is found in the social body rather than the larger cosmos.

Turner pushes the importance of the way rituals form and nourish relationships even further. He says that rituals reveal the structure of *communitas* to the participants in the rituals. "*Communitas*," asserts Turner, "is the primal ground ... of social structure." Chihamba (another Ndembu ritual) "is an attempt to transmit to Ndembu the inherited wisdom of their culture about this primal ground of (social) experience, thought, and social action ...".[15]

The second new emphasis in Turner's ritual theory is the

multivalence of ritual gestures and symbols. Turner has shown how particular symbols and actions in rituals can mean different things, depending on their context and sequence. Especially through his work with the Ndembu, he found that a ritual gesture or instrument did not have a generalized (much less universal) meaning outside a particular social context or ritual order. The Ndembu practice of basket divination, in which a diviner used the tossing of a number of ritual objects around in a basket and a rigorous discipline of questions and answers from the concerned parties to determine the source of some unfortunate event, illustrated his point. He found that the people involved, the constellation of symbols and actions, and the order of events could change the meaning of the ritual actions and objects. Although each of the objects in the basket carried meaning for the divination, the meaning of those objects could vary greatly, depending on who attended the ritual, what they said, and in what sequence the objects came to the top of the pile in the basket.

Turner did not reduce the reach of ritual meaning to the social dimensions, as Durkheim and to a certain extent Lévi-Strauss had done. But he did find most of its meaning there, not just in its revelation and nourishing of the *communitas*, but in its ability to address issues of small sub-units and larger regional factors. He also saw ritual actions processing larger natural events, such as disease, for the people.

Turner's observation of the multivalence of symbols and gestures challenges the notion of the universal occurrence and meaning of types of ritual action. With such an understanding of the significance of the context and specificity of ritual actions, it is very difficult to maintain that everyone's ritual actions mean the same thing.

Turner's work on meals illustrates this point. He observes how particular meals nourish particular social realities in specific circumstances and how meals sometimes help constitute the social body. But he is much less interested in the possibility that meals are an expression of the connection to the eternal sacred. Turner, a practicing Roman Catholic, actually made some observations about the significance of the contemporary Christian eucharist, and in doing so depended heavily on the notion of *communitas* he had described in his observations of the Ndembu. There is, then, a notion in Turner that meals can serve to nourish social reality in similar ways across some cultural boundaries.

If ritual is more concerned with nurturing social realities than expressing eternal truths, and if the character of that nurturing depends on the context and sequence of the ritual actions, what kind of effects does ritual have on particular social bodies? It is not enough to state that ritual has a primarily social field of reference and effect without characterizing the social effects of ritual specifically. Politics and business, for instance, also have a primarily social field of reference and effect, but one would want a definition of ritual that at least to a certain extent distinguishes ritual from business and politics (they do almost inevitably overlap somewhat). Perhaps the clearest thinking at this level is that of the historian of religion Jonathan Z. Smith.

A student and colleague of Eliade, Smith's first-hand knowledge seems to have allowed him to make the clearest appreciation and break from the master. In many cases Smith turns the notion and examples of the eternal sacred against themselves.[16]

Smith, in a stand relatively similar to Turner's, rejects the universal or generalized meaning of particular kinds of ritual actions. As he examines the great variety of rituals in the history of religions and in this century's anthropological field studies, the Eliadean affirmation that all similar ritual actions have similar meaning and function appears overdrawn.

Smith does not just recognize the multivalent character of ritual gestures and symbols. He proposes that ritual actions consist of elements that are particularly "empty" of general meaning and particularly capable of particular signals, depending on the context and character of the situation. It is not because trees and poles, for instance, mean something similar in many different cultural and historical situations that they are used in many different rituals around the world. Rather, trees and poles are all present in a variety of different rituals precisely because they can carry a number of different meanings. In striking contrast to Jung, Eliade, and Campbell – all of whom have waxed eloquent about the universal significance of trees in ritual and myth – Smith declares that it is just because the tree is an "empty" symbol (meaning that it can mean a great variety of things) that it makes for an effective ritual object. This allows, according to Smith, for such "empty" (or multivalent) symbols to change their meaning as a particular people transforms or adjusts the significance of the ritual.

It should be noted that Smith is intentionally provocative in his use of the term "empty." He has picked up the word "empty" from Protestant usage of the term in the seventeenth to nineteenth centuries, when Reformers in their anti-Catholic zeal maintained that ritual meant nothing and that belief was everything. Smith, as we will see, has no sympathy for these Protestant suggestions that rituals are "empty" of significance. He does, however, delight in turning the term on its head, and using it in a way that also undermines the Eliadean assertion that rituals are full of universal meaning. Perhaps the least helpful aspect of this playful label is that it could imply that ritual actions are arbitrary and their categories senseless.

For Smith, the definitional task related to ritual is not to discover types of universal ritual actions, but to characterize the kinds of effects the variety of "empty" ritual actions have in their particular settings. He has characterized ritual in general as having the following overlapping effects on the people involved:

1. A marking or noticing of an occurrence, pattern, or dynamic within a situation.[17] Ritual actions in general are done in order to call attention to something that has happened or is happening in the environs of the participants. That to which the ritual calls attention is usually problematic for the particular society. The ritual marking or noticing "does not solve the problem, overcome the incongruity, or

resolve the tension. Rather it results in thought. It is a testing of the adequacy and applicability of traditional patterns and categories to new situations and data in the hopes of achieving rectification."[18]

2. A perfecting or rationalizing of such noticed phenomena. Ritual notices events that have become problems for people, and holds them up in a constructed setting to explain them away or to make them look better. Smith's treatment of the classic ritual text on the slaughter of the Siberian bear cub illustrates clearly how he has departed from the perspective of universal meaning.

The ritual killing of the Siberian bear cub has been often seen by the Eliadean school as a typical example of the general action of sacrifice.[19] A. I. Hallowell describes how circumpolar peoples capture a young bear cub, raise it as a part of the village family, and then ceremonially slaughter it.[20] Smith's explanation contrasts strongly with the universalists who propose that in this ceremonial killing we have the basics of ritual sacrifice throughout the world and history.[21] Smith sees that ritual simply as a chance to perfect the hunting of bears. The ceremonial killing of the cub corrects, rationalizes, and perfects the many mistakes that happen in a real bear hunt. It is not an archetypal example of how religious sacrifice came into being (in fact Smith rejects the notion that there is a general phenomenon of sacrifice in ritual).

Ritual "provides the means for demonstrating that we know what ought to have been done, what ought to have taken place. But, by the fact that it is ritual action rather than everyday action, it demonstrates that we know 'what is the case.' Ritual provides an occasion for reflection and rationalization on the fact that what ought to have been done was not done, what ought to have taken place did not occur."[22]

3. An assertion of difference within the social body. Just as ritual notices the events that are somehow problematic and irreconcilable for a particular group, it also marks the differences between people within a particular social formation.

Its juxtaposition of "empty" but different gestures and symbols attracts expression of differences within the community. Different symbols standing side by side in a ritual come to express different populations or positions within the group. Here Smith also insists that ritual asserts these differences mainly in order for the social body to be able to work with them, rather than to overcome them. Living with difference is a particular skill that a social body needs to develop because of its inevitability. Ritual nourishes the social body, according to Smith, by providing occasion and appropriate containers for recognition of social difference.

An example is Smith's study of the way Near Eastern temple structures observed the different claims on society made by the king and the priesthood.[23] He demonstrates the care with which the ritual place and movement of kings was demarcated in the ancient Near Eastern temples. He shows how the seating and movement of the king within these temples helped with the on-going negotiation of the power balance between the priesthood and the monarchy in Near Eastern society. There was never a final solution to the different claims of power by the kings and priests, but the ritual movements and positioning within the temple provided the occasion to notice the differences and to think about them.

Ritual symbols allow for groups to recognize these differences without necessarily trying to resolve them. This, of course, is a very effective means of nourishing the group in which differences exist. Rather than try to come up with a common and final solution to the differences, the multivalent symbols of ritual keep allowing for indirect recognition of those differences. This allows each different sub-group to be recognized and for the group as a whole to work regularly on non-final, adaptive and constantly revised compromises. Final solutions to differences almost always lead to the elimination of valued different perspectives. Ongoing ritual recognition of differences tends to nourish the particular sub-groups.

This observation of difference through ritual can, of

course, also refer to the differences between those in the group doing the ritual and those outside. This function of ritual has also been addressed in detail by anthropologists of the last generation, in particular Mary Douglas.[24] Douglas has studied the ways ritual meals address these questions of group identity by providing a means of demarcating those inside and those outside.[25] That is, the ritual meal reinforces or clarifies the identity of those inside.

Smith does not seem to deny that ritual can function in this way relative to these differences, but he prefers to see the ritual as an active help to the insiders in the group in reflecting on and adjusting to their differences with the outside.

Smith and Turner, then, seem to have paid closer attention to the specifics of ritual than Eliade, Jung, and Campbell. They have expanded, corrected, and extended the earlier attempts to deal with the spectrum of ritual throughout the world.

Christian meals and ritual theory

The striking fit of this recent ritual theory as exemplified by Turner and Smith with the new data about first-century Christian meals should be clear. These recent developments in general ritual theory provide a very helpful frame in which to see the amazing diversity of Christian meal interpretations in the first century. And they help us integrate that diversity of origins of the eucharist with the challenges of liturgical renewal today.

We have seen how banquets in the first century are multivalent and/or "empty" events that brought a wide variety of both Christian and non-Christian concerns to expression. Although the Greco-Roman banquet did serve similar functions for different groups, it had a variety of meanings for different groups. It served to memorialize people who had died. It was the occasion for others to have philosophical discussions. For guilds and trade unions it was an expression of camaraderie. For families and neighbors it was a way to observe a holiday. For some religious groups

it was a secret act of membership. For other religious groups
the singing after the supper led to great ecstasy.

We were not able to give one general meaning to any
of the banquet symbols or gestures, but we were able to
characterize the kinds of effects the meal had on the various
Christian and non-Christian bodies. Those effects (e.g. the
recognition to membership, the establishment of rank) are
astonishingly close to those identified by Smith and to the
notion of *communitas* in Turner.

For instance, the cup at the meal of the community of the
Gospel of Mark became a kind of group pledge to follow
Jesus even to the point of martyrdom. On the other hand, the
drinking of the cup for Paul is a way of affirming unity
within a somewhat fragmented group. And in contrast to
both of these, the Didache seems to see the cup as an
association with a spiritual Israel when it alludes to the
"vine of David." In each case the gesture of taking the
cup after the supper has been transformed from a simple
libation in the name of a god into a rectification or rationalization relative to the particular aspect of *communitas* being
evoked.

Our inability to find theological constants in particular
gestures and symbols of the early Christian meals also raises
questions about how one could find a universal meaning in
the first-century Lord's Supper. Instead of an overarching
theological message in the first-century Christian meals, we
have found use of the common symbols of blessing the
bread, eating, washing feet, praying of the cup, discussion,
and singing in a multivalent manner. Each of the elements of
the meal are used by the particular community to notice
occurrences, mark differences, or rationalize problems
according to its situation. That meals have to do with these
expressions within a community is the only constant we have
been able to find.

The ritual symbols themselves in the first-century Christian
meals are multivalent enough to correspond to the meaning
of Smith's provocative label of "empty." It is important to
remember that it is just this multivalence of ritual categories

for Smith that allows these meals to nourish their particular social realities.

This clear manner in which the Lord's Suppers of the first century can be seen to nurture the social realities of their particular groups helps us to address the extraordinary variety of Christian eucharistic practice today and throughout history. Christian meals, then, do not need to be unified under some one universal meaning or message, but can be seen as consistent with both current ritual theory and first-century precedent in their ability to nourish specific and individual social realities. They nourish social reality in the eclectic and improvised manner that ritual in general does. There is not a general meaning or function even to the meal as such. Like all ritual, it can mark and notice, perfect and rationalize, and assert difference within the reality of the *communitas*.

Lest one conclude at this point that ritual actions are so multivalent that they can mean anything one wants them to mean, it is important to state that the constant frame of meaning is the social reality of those doing the ritual. The multivalence of the ritual symbols acts within and on the group's own community. Even though the multivalence or emptiness of the symbols enables the community to negotiate the differences within its social reality, one cannot conclude that the symbols are meaningless. They always have a particular meaning within the social reality of those doing the ritual.

To return, then, to the question at the beginning of the chapter. Since the meanings of eucharists depend on their social context and sequence, the question as to which of those meals (see pp. 89 and 90) are a eucharist is not answerable. We have seen that there was no single eucharistic meaning, practice, or function in the first century. To rule out any event because it does not correspond to the correct original theological interpretation misses the mark, because the first-century Christians themselves were clearly adding and subtracting theological significance throughout the first century.

To rule out one of the meals mentioned at the beginning of the chapter on the grounds that it does not fit the original practice is perhaps even more absurd. Practice seems to have varied substantially in the first century. But even more striking is the fact that many of the elements which were stable in the first-century meals do not exist in twentieth-century eucharists (e.g. the meal itself, the discussions, and the extensive drinking of wine).

If one wants to transform the question into which of the meals are functioning as rituals, then the answer will most probably be: each of them except the fast-food meal. All of the other meals have clear ritual functions, according to Turner and Smith.

The change in the wording of the New Guinea mass is itself both a recognition of the community of the indigenous culture, and an occasion to reflect on the difference between the European faith and the New Guinean. The continued bread cubes and grape juice of the Missouri Presbyterians affirms the stability of their upper-middle-class Protestant situation in middle America, and helps them rectify or rationalize any aberrations in their suburban setting. For Peter as for his Jewish sisters and brothers before and around him the meal served as a way to affirm the differences between Jewish and Gentile in that complex Mediterranean society.

The youth group's coke and doughnuts in the worship on Sunday morning is, of course, a clear invitation to that community to look at the differences between the youth and the adults. The harvest festival in Cameroun is the occasion to mark the passing of the rainy season and to notice the gathering harvest.

Theological dimensions to eucharistic theory

Having applied current ritual theory and New Testament research to issues of contemporary worship renewal, we note here that this has so far been done with little recourse to theological discourse. We have reflected upon the three arenas of first-century Christianity, the general subject of

ritual, and liturgical renewal today through the disciplines of
social analyses and literary criticisms. This has made for
some coherent associations between the three arenas. And it
has been done by and large without theological reflection.

There has been a strong assumption that Christian ritual,
often called liturgy or worship, involves encounter with
God. How does this assumption fit with what has been said
in this chapter? Are there ways of integrating theological
expression with the analysis and proposals of this book? How
can we speak of God in relationship to worship while making
use of the insights of our investigation so far?

The very notion of God especially present in the worship
service has been a theological problem for Christians for
some time. If worship is where one encounters God, is God
not anywhere else? This idea that God or Christ are especially
present in the bread, wine, sanctuary, or worship-hour seem
to privilege worship as a place and time for God.

As such they run counter to the main theologies of
creation, history, and incarnation. A faith that affirms God's
creative presence in nature and the universe cannot posit that
liturgy is a privileged locus of the divine. A God who
"pervades and permeates all things" through the activity of
creation (Wisdom 7:24) is no more revealed in worship than
in the budding of a flower.

Similarly, the God who is revealed in the history of Israel
and/or in all of human history cannot be in some way limited
by the worship service. Nor does the God who became
incarnate in Jesus and/or humanity through Jesus point to
liturgy as a special locus for human-divine encounter. This
God has been proclaimed as visible in all of history, human
life, and creation.

So implicitly theology has asked for another definition of
worship. Theology itself has needed a way of thinking about
worship which did not privilege worship theologically,
because the basic Christian doctrines have affirmed a God
who is revealed primarily elsewhere. Theological reflection
on worship has needed to join the mainstreams of Christian
theologies of incarnation, creation, and history. We believe

that the integration of the data, theory, and analysis presented here can contribute substantially toward meeting this long-standing need for a revised theology of worship.

How, then, might we begin to talk about God and liturgy coherently within the frame of the program of liturgical renewal and analysis outlined in this book? We suggest three possible ways to theologize about worship without abandoning the critical and creative perspectives gained in what has been said up to now.

It should be noted that these are three different approaches which are not compatible with one another. They are three different ways of talking about God while integrating the perspectives of this book. They are exploratory. Because critical analysis of ritual is now making its way into the sphere of the churches, these are not fully developed theologies, but initial attempts at theologizing about worship from this new perspective.

1. God as community

The first way has been keynoted by Victor Turner himself. Essentially, Turner suggests that ritual does point to God, inasmuch as we associate God and community. Since ritual nourishes community, it orients people toward God.

After observing the ways in which ritual is fundamentally connected to *communitas*, Turner says, "*communitas* may be regarded as the 'Godhead' underlying Emile Durkheim's 'God,' in the sense that Durkheim's 'God' was a shorthand for all social-structural actualities and possibilities, while 'Godhead' (though not too distant from Durkheim's 'effervescence') is the performative *communitas* reality from which all social structures may be endlessly generated."[26]

In other words, inasmuch as ritual nourishes and connects with *communitas*, from Turner's and Durkheim's point of view, one can speak of ritual pointing to God. It is important to note that the ways in which this sociologist and anthropologist speak of God are quite different from traditional Christian theology. But inasmuch as one can conceive of God as "all social-structural actualities and possibilities" and

"Godhead" as the "performative *communitas* reality from which all social structures may be endlessly generated," one can see a way of integrating Turner's categories and theological language.

We should not be put off by the density of Turner's language. This can also be expressed in the perhaps more familiar terms of Christian piety. For many Christians, God is made known primarily in the assembled community. For instance, "the body of Christ" often symbolizes the community of Christians in liturgical usage. God in the body of Christ is encountered primarily in the community of the faithful. Therefore if liturgy from the point of view of ritual theory nourishes and maintains the community, it can be seen as a primary means to God.[27]

This is no longer a God outside the universe, but one penetrating and identifying its generative fibers. This God is the actualization of human community in its broadest and deepest sense. If ritual nurtures social reality in the particular way each community needs, then ritual does have a special relationship to the *communitas*-God.

To a certain extent, this theological approach does privilege ritual (and therefore liturgy and eucharist) theologically. Inasmuch as God is primarily community, and community is nourished in a special way by ritual, ritual points in a central way to God.

2. God as multivalent

Another way of theologizing about God and worship within our framework is to note that the term "God" is one of those multivalent symbolic terms used in ritual. Such terms, as we have seen, attach themselves to particular aspects of the social reality of a group so that that group may re-experience the particular social issues at hand.

From this perspective "God" and "Christ" are extremely helpful multivalent ritual categories that are available to communities to express themselves on a variety of on-going social dynamics. It is precisely the multivalence or "emptiness" of these theological terms that makes them especially appropriate to ritual usage. Because "God" can mean so many different things, it is precisely the kind of apparatus which ritual needs to continue to process events in the community.

"God" can be both the ritual subject for the pietist Protestant as she approaches the kneeling rail for communion and at a different time the ritual category for the same person's expression of allegiance to her country. Ritual does not pretend to be logical or consistent in its use of gestures or language. So "God" can be the category which both allows an individual to reflect at the communion rail on a dispute with her son and calls for feelings of loyalty for the United States of America when the pledge of allegiance is said.

This also can be said in terms of Christian piety. God encompasses many different realities. Not all of them are always available to all human beings. And God comes to different people in different ways. In worship, then, God can mean different things to different people, because God is so many different things.

3. God in all things, including worship

A final way of thinking about God and liturgy within the frame of this book radically relativizes the theological significance of liturgy. If God is present in all creation and history, then God could be seen as at work in worship also. This "presence," however, would not be in any way theologically different from, or privileged over, God's presence in the process of electing a president of Nicaragua, in the growth of a tomato, or in the crash of a meteor into Neptune.

Such a perspective values God in ritual as a part of God's presence and work in all of the universe. Ritual can be divine inasmuch as it reveals a part of God's being. In such a view, any dogmatic or ethical qualifications on the presence of God in the universe in general would apply to God's presence in worship. In other words, if in Christian belief God is love, then God is especially present in all acts of love in the universe. Similarly, this God would be especially present in acts of worship that are loving and absent in ones that were not.

With regard to Smith's three characterizations of ritual as marking occurrences, rationalizing or perfecting them, and recognizing differences, it is easy to see a Christian God in the first and the third actions. One can understand a Christian God as being active in making people conscious of events and in helping people to recognize and observe differences. It is more problematic to see a Christian God active in the human process of rationalizing mistakes or oversights.

From this perspective, then, God would be present, but not in a privileged way, whenever events were brought to consciousness or whenever differences were respected. Of course, these occur both in and beyond ritual. God would then be present and active in those rituals where difference was respected, in the same way that God would be present when differences were respected outside rituals. It would be important to remember that rituals, and in our case eucharists, deal in a kind of discourse that seems especially good at respecting differences and processing important or problematic events.

In this theological perspective, ritual and worship would be valued in relationship to God, but not in any privileged manner. Worship would be divine inasmuch as it represented that part of God which nourishes community through recognition of difference and recollection of important and problematic events.

This theological approach also can be put in terms of Christian piety. In this perspective God meets people in the forest, at work, in family, during sexual intercourse, in the classroom, in day-dreams, and in worship. Every aspect of creation is God's dwelling-place, including the moments and locations for eucharists. But when family, day-dreams, sex, or work violate God's love or justice, it may be that God is not encountered where one expects God. In a similar way, when worship and the eucharist violate God's love or justice in some way, Christians, like Amos of the Hebrew scriptures, may hear God say: "I hate, I despise your feast days. I take no pleasure in your solemn assemblies . . . But let justice roll down like water, and righteousness like a mighty stream" (Amos 5:21, 24).

· 6 ·

Eucharistic Liturgies for Different Social Settings Today

This chapter contains six real Christian table events, each of which we see as being within the traditions of the eucharist, although not all of them would meet everyone's criteria for these events. These worship services all are different, depending on their social settings. Many of their social settings are broad enough to be usable in some of the readers' settings.

These are not presented primarily as a sampler of contemporary eucharists, although readers are encouraged to use them where appropriate. The main purpose in presenting them is to illustrate the thesis of the book in a contemporary setting. We want to demonstrate in some detail that the process of adjusting a eucharist in order to give expression to a particular social reality of the group involved can be advanced in the late twentieth century. It is important to observe here that our main eucharistic traditions today no longer resemble a real meal, nor is our worship any longer held at table. Rather, our worship gatherings have developed their own "social codes" and formats. There are some meal dimensions left to our current eucharistic formats, but for the meal to be the primary context for the eucharist today would require the kind of wholesale alteration that most churches would not consider.

So in the presentation of each liturgy, we will outline the particular social setting and issues that the eucharist addressed. In addition, we will show how the particular eucharists were developed in and for those settings and issues. And we will make suggestions about use of this liturgical material today.

I. A eucharistic celebration of summer

Observations and instructions

This eucharist has been created for a regular Sunday morning service of an urban congregation. It probably can apply as well to churches in suburban and rural settings.

More crucial are two other factors. First of all, it is for people who are experiencing the warmth and growth of summer. It would be bizarre to celebrate this service in the dead of winter. Its success depends on its addressing people's experience of summer.

Secondly, it is for those who are aware of ecological and evolutionary dynamics in their situation. That is, it means to help people integrate their relationship with nature, especially in its growth and productivity, with culture and the Christian faith.

In his recent work, *The Coming of the Cosmic Christ*, Matthew Fox has noted how much of Christian tradition has overlooked the basic biblical message of creation in favor of an emphasis on redemption.[1] Fox points out that spirituality for our day will depend more and more on human consciousness of the connectedness between nature, God, and people.

It is in the interest of such integration that this eucharistic liturgy is offered. It has been used especially to help Christians integrate an affirmation of their connection to nature into their faith.

The liturgy

This liturgy contains an opening litany and a prayer of consecration at the table. Other elements of the eucharistic liturgy may go according to the normal procedure of the particular congregation.

OPENING LITANY

People (*singing*): **You send your breath.**
And they come to life.
You give the earth the bloom of youth.

Leader 1: In the early spring, pale green blades of wheat broke through the earth's surface.

Leader 2: This hand of mine began to take shape millions of years ago as the first leaves stretched out for nourishment and light.

Leader 3: Eons ago the earth itself was glowing with heat as it separated itself from the sun.

People (*singing*): **You send your breath.**
And they come to life.
You give the earth the bloom of youth.

Leader 1: By mid-summer the wheat stems sway heavily

in the breeze for miles and miles of green and golden earth.

Leader 2: The early species of deer, able to move quickly and nimbly in a way we can only imitate, learned which plants were best for them to eat and sought them out.

Leader 3: The ground we stand on carries in it the remnants of volcanos and oceans which once dominated the landscape.

People: **You send your breath.**
And they come to life.
You give the earth the bloom of youth.

Leader 1: This morning we gather around the bread, which comes from the wheat in the fields.

Leader 2: This morning we celebrate our oneness with the plants and the animals, which precede and surround us.

Leader 3: This morning we remember that we are earth people, united with each other and to all on this globe by the ground under us.

Leaders: One body, one history, one home for us all.

People: **You send your breath.**
And they come to life.
You give the earth the bloom of youth.

Leaders: One body, one history, one home for us all.

People: **You send your breath.**
And they come to life.
You give the earth the bloom of youth.

SILENT PRAYER

People: **You send your breath.**
And they come to life.
You give the earth the bloom of youth.

OTHER LITURGICAL ACTS (e.g. Sermon, Prayers, Songs)

PRAYER OF CONSECRATION

Celebrant: Life grows from the earth. The kernel of wheat lives in the soil before it breaks ground. As it stretches itself skyward it also reaches deeper into the earth. Water and nourishment blend with sunlight as the stalk begins to produce kernels of its own. This bread holds those kernels, that sunshine, that soil and water. As we take it into ourselves, we affirm our own roots in the earth. (*Holding the bread up*) This is the ground we stand upon, the earth yearning to be inside us, the body of Christ. (*Breaking bread*) It is the life we have taken in order to live ourselves. Life broken for us all.

Life flows toward us from the Source beyond us. It is a stream that creates us anew each day. It is a stream that wants to make its way through us. A stream that flows through the city and country. A stream that readies a harvest in every season. (*Holding up the cup*) This is the life we have received from the earth and from our forbearers. This is the pulsing energy that has made a home in us and that we give on, the blood of Christ.

APPROPRIATE CONCLUSIONS ACCORDING TO LOCAL OR
DENOMINATIONAL PRACTICE

II. Table fellowship: an informal community pot-luck

Observations and instructions

The kind of setting for this service may vary a great deal. It can be for both a local church group or for a broader mix of people from church and community. The room setting is typically a church fellowship hall. The occasion is a real meal together.

The major set of issues that this eucharist addresses are those of groups of people needing to get to know one another better, experience their differences within a supportive setting, or resolve some implicit disputes among them. For instance, the situation described in Chapter 3, pp. 78–9, is an appropriate setting for this service.

The way this eucharist came into being, not just in the congregations we have been associated with, but in many others, seems to be through the need for a setting where informality and structure mixed in ways that allowed for getting to know one another and experiencing differences in the congregation. Almost always, this was expressed in terms of the congregation's need to have more time together as people. In many cases, pastoral awareness of the first-century meal traditions of the early churches accounted for the insertion of the eucharistic or other prayer words. This element of the services seems to have come from both a need by most everyone to endorse or bless the social processes and a need for the pastor to assert her/his role in such processes.

The liturgy

As noted above, this service is set within a real meal of the congregation held in a church fellowship hall or a similar space. Typically the food is provided by the members bringing some prepared dish from home. All of these different food offerings are then placed on common tables, and people serve themselves in a buffet manner before sitting down at tables around the room.

There are three different sets of prayers and gestures that can be done during the meal.

The first is:

At the beginning of the meal before the people approach the tables for food, the pastor welcomes everyone. She/he then takes a loaf of bread and says:

"The tradition I received from the Lord is that on the night he was handed over, the Lord Jesus took some bread, and after he had given thanks, he broke it, and he said, 'This is my body, which is for you. Do this in remembrance of me'" (I Corinthians 11:23, 24). So let us now give thanks for what God has given us. Are there things for which you are thankful this evening? After each item someone mentions, let us all say together, "Thanks be to God".

The pastor waits for people to mention some of these things and leads the congregation in the response. Then the pastor concludes with a brief prayer of thanksgiving for those present.

Then the people take their food and eat together at the various tables.

Near the end of the meal, the pastor stands up and asks that someone from each table makes sure that everyone has a glass of wine (or grape juice, if that is the eucharistic custom of the congregation). When all have something in their cups, then she/he says: "After the supper, Jesus took the cup, saying, 'This cup is the new covenant in my blood. Whenever you drink it, do it as a memorial to me.' Amen."

The pastor asks for a few moments of silence. Then he/she lets everyone know that they may linger as long as they want at the table, but that there will be no more formal time together.

The second way of setting words and prayers within this meal is to have the words of consecration over the bread and the cup at the same time. In this case they both would be said near the end of the meal, after people had finished eating. This would mean that each table at the pot-luck would also have a ceremonial distribution of bread at the end of the meal after the words of consecration are said.

The third variation would be not to say the traditional Last Supper words at all, but to have different prayers that are more group-oriented. This has been done in the following manner. At the beginning of the meal, the pastor or other worship leader greets everyone. Then he/she asks that everyone think of one thing for which they are thankful. The worship leader then asks for any persons who wish, to speak their thanksgiving out loud, and for the congregation to respond "Thanks be to God" after each person says something. Then the worship leader closes with "Amen."

Again, near the end of the meal the worship leader asks for everyone's attention. At this point she/he asks that everyone think of people or issues about which they are concerned and for which they would like to pray, and that after each person speaks the congregation say, "Hear our prayer, O God." At the end of this time the worship leader closes the time of prayer with a benediction. After the benediction the leader encourages people to stay around the tables if they wish.

III. Manna for the desert: a eucharistic celebration of Black history

Observations and instructions

This worship service blends images from Black American history and the Bible, and sets them within a eucharist. In doing so, it integrates thanksgiving for the courage and creativity of American Black persons into the two primary elements of Christian tradition.

It is important to observe that although there are many Black persons in American and English churches, the general liturgy and the eucharist in particular has very little place for the recognition of traditions and history that are not Anglo-Saxon, German, or Latin. The shape of the liturgy assumes and images a preference for the ways the white persons in Europe and America have lived and worshipped. Even though both America and England now have many settings in which Black and white persons work, live, and/or worship together, the churches show little recognition of the diversity now present in both cultures. This liturgy has addressed quite directly the need for incorporation of Black history and tradition into worship.

This liturgy was composed for an integrated congregation's celebration of Black history month. It was celebrated twice each February for approximately eight years in that church. It has also been used in other integrated and largely Black settings. And it has been used at other times of the year than Black history month.

Several times after having participated in this liturgy, visiting Roman Catholics have asked whether this was a eucharist or not. It should be noted that the words of consecration are not those of the Last Supper, and that much, although not all, of the wording of the mass is missing. This is, of course, the *question* addressed seriously in this book, especially in Chapter 5.

This liturgy is meant to stand in the larger table tradition of Christianity. In the sense of our use of the term "eucharist" as the various table traditions in primitive Christianity, this can clearly be considered one.

But it is conceivable that labeling it a "eucharist" could prevent it from being used in certain church settings because of its lack of the traditional words of institution. In such cases we recommend that it not be considered a formal eucharist so that the congregation, by not calling it a "eucharist", may experience this important blending of Black history, the Bible, and the table traditions of Christianity. It should be clear by this point that "eucharist" and "Lord's Supper" have had diverse definitions since the beginning, and that therefore the name of the event is less crucial than how it nourishes the particular community in which it is celebrated.

The liturgy

In the worship order given here place has been left for songs, hymns, prayers for the day, and sermon. This service may be done without a sermon, but in keeping with the importance of the sermon within the Black churches a sermon is recommended. Some particular recommended songs and hymns have been noted here, but these may be replaced.

INVOCATION

God brought the people out of Egypt. On the banks of the sea Miriam, the prophetess, took the timbrel and led the people in dance and praise to God for delivering the people from slavery. Then the people had to travel through the desert toward the promised land. The way was hard, there was little to eat and drink, and the people began to complain. God heard their complaint, and caused bread to come down from heaven to feed them daily. They called this bread manna, and they had enough to eat during all the time they were in the desert.

SILENT PRAYER

FREEDOM

Leader: When Kunta Kinte was taken slave in Gambia, he fought back, struggling until he was unconscious.

People: **The one who eats my flesh and drinks my blood, Jesus said, lives in me and I live in that one.**

Leader: When men denied rights to women, Sojourner Truth proclaimed proud personhood.

People: **God saved them from the grasp of those who hated them.**

Leader: When discrimination continued throughout the nation, Marcus Garvey pointed to noble African roots.

People: **God divided the sea and brought the people through.**

Leader: When university doors were closed, James Meredith marched.

People: **My flesh is real food, Jesus said, and my blood is real drink.**

Leader: When the war machine robbed the nation of people and funds, Martin Luther King Jr stood strong against the American government.

People: **Whoever eats my flesh, Jesus said, draws life from me.**

Leader: When society worried about its possessions, Julia Jameson did a proud dance of freedom.

People: **And the waters swallowed their oppressors.**

Leader: Amen.

People: **Amen.**

HYMN "Lift Every Voice and Sing" (recommended)

DESERT

Leader: In the fall of 1979 Ku Klux Klan members shot and killed peaceful demonstrators in North Carolina.

People: (*singing*) **Lord, have mercy. Christ, have mercy. Lord, have mercy.**

Leader: Thirty-five years after the Supreme Court ruling against segregation, most classrooms are still segregated.

People: (*singing*) **Lord, have mercy. Christ, have mercy. Lord, have mercy.**

Leader: Today the rate of unemployment for minorities ranges between two and five times as much as for the rest of the nation.

People: (*singing*) **Lord, have mercy. Christ, have mercy. Lord, have mercy.**

HYMN "There is a Balm in Gilead" (recommended)

DOUBT

A READING OF PSALM 22 *Remembering the Martyrs*

(to be read in unison)
My God, my God, why have you deserted me?
I call all day long, my God, but you never answer.
In you our ancestors put their trust.
They called to you and they were saved.
Yet, here I am, more worm than person.
All who see me jeer at me.
Yet you drew me out of the womb.
You entrusted me to my mother's breasts.
Do not stand aside, trouble is near.
A herd of bulls surround me.
Their jaws are agape for me, like lions tearing and roaring.
I remember the martyrs who preceded us, the slaves who died on ships carrying them to America.
I am like water draining away.
My heart is like wax, melting inside me.
They divide my garments among them, and cast lots for my clothes.
I remember the martyrs who preceded us, the lynch victims of the past two centuries.
Do not stand aside, God.
Rescue my soul from the sword.
Save me from the lion's mouth.
I remember Malcolm X, martyr for justice.
You are the theme of my praise in the great assembly.
The poor will receive as much as they want to eat.

I remember Martin Luther King Jr, martyr for freedom.
The whole earth will remember and come back to God.
And God's justice will be proclaimed to a people yet unborn.

SCIPTURE READINGS

SERMON/HOMILY

PRAYERS OF THE CHURCH

MANNA

Leader: God is with you.
People: **And also with you.**
Leader: Look at the desert around you.
People: **We have lived through grace and suffering.**
Leader: Jesus said, I am the bread of life.
      The one who comes to me will never be hungry.
      The one who believes in me will never thirst.
      Whoever comes to me, I will not turn away.
People: **In the desert when God's children were hungry and disoriented, God rained down manna from heaven to help them on their way.**
Leader: In this place God Sabaoth will prepare a banquet for all peoples.
People: **God has seen the mourning of the people. God has confronted the death that surrounds us.**
Leader: This is the bread that comes down from heaven, Jesus said, and the bread which I give is my flesh for the life of the world.
People: **I have a dream that one day my children will live in a nation where they are judged according to their character and not according to the color of their skin.**
Leader: (*raising bread and cup*): On that day it will be said, See this is our God.
People: **Those who eat my flesh and drink my blood, Jesus said, live in me and I in them.**
Leader: And the manna the children ate in the desert was sweet like honey.
People: **For my flesh is real food, and my blood is real drink, Jesus said.**

DISTRIBUTION OF BREAD AND CUP (*It is recommended that the song "Kum Bay Yah" be sung here*).

CLOSING LITANY AND BENEDICTION

Leader: The shame of God's people has been removed.

People: **Let freedom ring from the high Alleghenies of Pennsylvania.**

Leader: God will wipe away the tears from every cheek.

People: **Let freedom ring from Georgia's Stone Mountain. Let freedom ring from every hill and molehill in Mississippi.**

Leader: Amen.

People: **Amen.**

IV. A house eucharist

Observations and instructions

The setting for this eucharist is a private home. Most often it is attended by the people who live in the home and others from the neighborhood, church, or extended family. The words and gestures of this service are almost always as close to those which occur in the church as possible. It is the change of location that expresses a major different social message in this eucharist.

The issues and larger social factors in this eucharist have to do mostly with the decline of the institutions of church and home. By placing a service that usually in our cultures occurs in a church into a home, one helps the people involved safely note and adjust to the fact that the church's influence, scope of activity, and constituency is dwindling. At the same time, it is a gesture of support and recognition to the particular home and the enterprise itself of being a home. Very often, the home setting ends up being in some way one that is not what one imagines as typical (e.g. person living alone, child or parent missing for one reason or other, presence of non-nuclear family person). The hosting of the house eucharist serves as a recognition of the "untypical" arrangement by an outside body and a "revelation" of that arrangement by those in the home.

Often these house eucharists are initiated as a way of recruiting neighbors, family members, or lapsed church-goers themselves. It is our experience that although on some level this may be one of the generative mechanisms for the service, it hardly ever functions as such. These house eucharists do not seem to draw people back into the church organization very successfully. They do seem to be successful as ways of helping people adjust to the new roles of church and home.

The liturgy

It is important that the eucharistic liturgy said in the home is as close to the one in the church as possible. Of course, some adjustments, especially around the music, are neces-sary. But for the service to nourish the family and the church in the ways mentioned above, it is important that the eucharistic liturgy of the particular church come into the home.

For this reason we do not print one standard liturgy here, but recommend that the resources of the particular church and denomination be used.

It should be clear that the atmosphere will be quite different. By and large such house eucharists are much more informal in their mood. But it is just this striking difference in mood that helps this service nourish people. The recognition of the difference between home and church, between expectation of family constellation and the reality, and the hope generated by the liturgy being said in a relatively full room (rather than a relatively empty church) all come from the built-in contrast created by keeping the liturgical words and gestures as similar as possible. This tension then in turn creates dramatic turns in the feeling of the people about both their church and their home, and accomplishes the nurture of the particular social reality.

V. Wisdom's table: two inclusive eucharistic prayers of consecration

Observations and instructions

The last two decades have witnessed the awakening of many congregations, and especially women within those congregations, to the need for inclusive language. It has been pointed out that the church's language in referring to people and to God is heavily weighted with masculine references. Both God and humanity are described as male in most church and liturgical language. According both to psychological studies and to the testimony of many church women, such exclusively male references disenfranchise many women. The lack of reference to humans or God as female makes women invisible in many worship situations. It of course also robs the congregation of a sense of equality in worship or a chance to work on the meaning of gender difference within a vision of equality.

This problem is especially acute relative to the eucharist. Since the churches have focused so much on the Last Supper and since Jesus himself was a male, the celebration of the eucharist has been dominated by the presence of a man. In the words of a clergy woman, "When I was celebrating the eucharist ... I kept asking myself, 'What am I doing? Celebrating the experience of some man? What does he have to do with me?' ... I felt silly passing out the body and blood of a man. All of my theological grounding gave way. And I kept trying to talk myself out of it: 'But you know that in Christ there is no male or female – you know that the body of Christ includes us all.' But it made no difference. All I could see was that this central act of the church was the celebration of the life, death, and resurrection of a man – and I felt outside."[2]

The two eucharistic prayers of consecration which follow are attempts to make the eucharist a more inclusive event for women and men. These prayers do so by making reference both to Jesus and to the biblical figure of Wisdom, who is represented throughout scripture as a female persona and who is closely associated with Jesus in the New Testament. In other words, these eucharistic prayers do not remove Jesus and his maleness from the eucharist. Rather they add Wisdom and her femaleness.[3] This inclusive approach matches the symbols of the eucharist nicely in that Jesus is associated with the bread and Wisdom with the cup.

This reference to both Jesus and Wisdom helps the congregation stay together in the ritual itself while enabling the recognition of the differences between men and women.

Both of these prayers were generated in a congregation where there was a strong feminist presence. Both have since been used in a number of other congregations with less feminist leanings. The strong emphasis on biblical quotations in them allows them to be used in settings in which feminist consciousness is not strong, but in which inclusive spirituality may be of help.

The liturgies

Both of these prayers of consecration can be attached to any eucharistic celebration. Because the first one uses the entire "words of institution" formula of the traditional eucharists, it is very usable in almost any church. Many denominations, including the Roman Catholic Church, recognize a variety of prayers of consecration within a set liturgy.

PRAYER OF CONSECRATION A

Leader (*taking bread*): On the night in which he was betrayed Jesus took bread. After giving you thanks, he broke the bread. After giving you thanks, he broke the bread, gave it to the disciples and said, "Take, eat, this is my body which is given for you." When the supper was over, he took the cup. Again he gave thanks to you, O God, gave the cup to the disciples and said, "Drink from this, all of you, this is the cup of the new covenant in my blood, poured out for you and for many, for the forgiveness of sins." When we eat this bread and drink this cup, we experience anew the presence of Jesus with us.

People: **You are the image of the unseen God,**
the firstborn of all creation.
In you all things were created,
everything visible and everything invisible (from
Colossians 1).
You bring forth food from the earth and wine to
cheer our hearts.
How great you are, clothed in majesty and
splendor (from Psalm 104:1, 14).

Leader (*taking cup*): Wisdom has built herself a house.
She has slaughtered her beasts, drawn her wine.
She has set her table.
She says: "Come, eat of my bread. Drink the wine I have
prepared" (Proverbs 9: 1, 2, 5)

People: **You exist before all things.**
and you hold all things together (from Colossians
1).
Your open hand fills us with what we need.
Turn away your face and we panic.
Send out your breath and life begins.
You renew the face of the earth (from Psalm
104:29, 30).

PRAYER OF CONSECRATION B

Leader: Wisdom has built herself a house,
She has hewn her seven pillars,
She has slaughtered her beasts, drawn her wine.

People: **She has laid her table.**
She has despatched her maidservants
and proclaimed from the heights of the city:

Leader: Come and eat of my bread.

People: **Drink the wine which I have drawn for you**
(Proverbs 9:1–3, 5).

Leader: Jesus said, "The Son of Man came, eating and
drinking, and they say, Look a glutton and a drunkard, a
friend of tax collectors and sinners." Yet Wisdom is
justified by her deeds (Matthew 11:19).

People: **For Wisdom is true to her name.**

**Put your feet into her fetters,
and your neck into her collar;
Offer your shoulder to her burdens,
Do not be impatient of her bonds.**

Leader: Court her with all your soul,
and with all your might keep in her ways.
Search for her, track her down, she will reveal herself.
Once you hold her, do not let her go.

People: **For in the end you will find rest in her
and she will take the form of joy for you;
Her fetters you will find a mighty defense.
Her yoke will be a golden ornament** (Ecclesiasticus
6:22a, 23–30).

Leader (*breaking bread*): Jesus said, "Come unto me, all you
who labor and are overburdened, and I will give you rest.
Shoulder my yoke and learn from me, for I am gentle and
humble in heart, and you will find rest for your souls."

People: **"Yes, my yoke is easy and my burden is light"**
(Matthew 11:28, 29).

Leader (*taking the cup*): Her bonds will be purple ribbons;
You will wear her like a robe of honor,
You will put her on like a crown of joy (Ecclesiasticus
6:30, 31).

People: **Yes, Wisdom is justified by her deeds** (Matthew
11:19).

VI. A service of eucharistic presence for the Easter season

Observations and instructions
The following eucharistic liturgy makes use of biblical
material about Jesus at table, but makes no reference to the
Last Supper tradition. As such it is an important illustration
of the statements in Chapters 3 and 4 concerning Christian
"eucharistic" traditions which are outside the frame of
reference of the Last Supper.

The setting for this service may be almost any Protestant
congregation. It was generated in a Protestant congregation

with a substantial number of lapsed Roman Catholics, and may be more appropriate to such settings. It also could be incorporated into a Roman Catholic mass, but would probably not have the same effect.

The issues addressed here are those related to Protestant-Catholic relations in our day. The service uses Easter biblical texts to evoke a sense of Jesus' presence at the contemporary Lord's table. That is, it uses what is typically Protestant material to make what is typically Catholic theology by focusing on the astounding parallel of resurrection and meal in a number of the New Testament texts. As such it addresses the sense of difference between Roman Catholics and Protestants within both denominations and in a world where interaction and co-operation is increasing. It relativizes those differences that Catholics and Protestants experience. It acknowledges both positions and gives final endorsement to neither. It presents a provisional occasion in which Protestants (and lapsed or alienated Catholics) can observe their increasing relatedness and put their own loyalties in perspective.

It could be possible that the liturgy could have a similar effect in a Roman Catholic mass. The problem is that in many Roman Catholic situations the requirements for a standard and approved form for the mass are strong enough to rule out the possible use of this material.

This service was generated by both an increasing Roman Catholic presence in the Protestant congregation in question and a more general agenda, especially of the pastor, to address issues of ecumenicity. As this Protestant congregation became more mixed, it seemed important for the body as a whole to notice and embrace the different denominational backgrounds in the body as a whole.

This eucharistic service fits most closely with the liturgical season of Eastertide. It has been used as an Easter Sunday service, but also as a service during the following Sundays of Eastertide.

An important element of the service is the sung response. This is a new song for congregations. The song itself should be practiced ahead of time, preferably just before the worship service and with the help of a choir.

The liturgy

Here again the major new elements of the liturgy are the initial litanies and the prayer of consecration. In this case a proposed order of the rest of the worship is also given, but congregations are encouraged to place the litanies and prayer of consecration in the appropriate spots in their own liturgies, should they have a substantially different order.

OPENING LITANY

Leader: They gathered in the room around the table, where they had heard the call.

People: **They were discouraged, because all that they had lived for was gone.**

Leader: And suddenly they were aware of Jesus among them again.

People: **Just as when he had broken bread with them before.**

People (*singing*): **I stand here knocking,**
Knock – one, two, three, four.
If you hear me knocking,
If you open the door,
I will come in
I'll eat with you there
Sit at your table.
You'll eat with me too.

Heath Allen

in   I'll eat with you   there   Sit at your

ta - ble   You'll eat with me too.

(music by Heath Allen, words by Heath Allen as paraphrase of Revelation 3:20).

OPENING HYMN

LITANY

Leader: In the evening of that same day, the first day of the week, the doors were closed in the room, and the disciples were together. Jesus came to them and said, "Peace be with you."

People (*singing*): **I stand here knocking.**
     Knock – one, two, three, four.
     If you hear me knocking,
     If you open the door,
     I will come in.
     I'll eat with you there.
     Sit at your table.
     You'll eat with me too.

Leader: After walking together with the stranger, they sat down with him and ate. When he broke the bread, they knew that Jesus was risen.

People (*singing*): **I stand here knocking,**
     Knock – one, two, three, four.
     If you hear me knocking,
     If you open the door,
     I will come in.
     I'll eat there with you.
     Sit at your table.
     You'll eat with me too.

SCRIPTURE LESSONS

SERMON/HOMILY

CONCERNS OF THE CHURCH

PRAYER OF THE CHURCH

PASSING OF THE PEACE

OFFERTORY

THE RESURRECTION MEAL (PRAYER OF CONSECRATION):

Leader: As they came ashore from fishing, there was someone there with bread, standing by the fire.

People: **In the room behind closed doors Jesus appeared
at the table after his death.**

Leader: On the lonely road he appeared to them

People: **And at the table they recognized him.**

Leader: God is with you.

People: **And also with you.**

Leader: Lift up your hearts.

People: **We lift them up to God.**

Leader: Let us remember how Jesus' victory over death was
made known to the disciples in the breaking of bread.

People: **It is right to give God thanks and praise.**

Leader: Holy One, we hold up the moments when Jesus
appeared to the disciples after his death. He took bread.
After giving you thanks, he broke the bread and gave it to
those around him.

People: (*singing*) **I stand here knocking,**
        Knock – one, two, three, four.
        If you hear me knocking,
        If you open the door,
        I will come in
        I'll eat there with you.
        Sit at your table.
        You'll eat with me too.

Leader: When we eat this bread and drink this cup, we
experience anew the presence of the Lord Jesus Christ and
look forward to his coming in final victory.

People: **Christ has died.**
        Christ has risen.
        Christ will come again.

Leader: We remember and proclaim, O God, what Jesus has done for us in this life and death, in his resurrection and ascension. Send the power of your Holy Spirit on us, gathered here out of love for you, and on these gifts. Help us know in the breaking of this bread and the drinking of this wine the presence of Christ.

People: **Make us one with Christ, one with each other, and one in service to all.**

As the celebrant breaks the bread and holds up the cup the people sing.

People (*singing*): **I stand here knocking,
Knock – one, two, three, four.
If you hear me knocking,
If you open the door,
I will come in
I'll eat there with you.
Sit at your table.
You'll eat with me too.**

THE DISTRIBUTION

CLOSING HYMN

BENEDICTION AND SENDING FORTH

Notes

1. Worship at a Crossroad

1. First published in Philip Larkin, *The Less Deceived* (Hessle, Yorkshire: Marvell Press 1955) 28f.
2. David Timms, *Philip Larkin* (The Modern Writers Series, New York: Harper & Row 1973), 81.
3. *Baptism, Eucharist and Ministry* (Faith and Order Paper No. 111, Geneva: World Council of Churches 1982).
4. Ibid., p. viii.
5. Geoffrey Wainwright, "Introduction" to "Liturgies of the Eucharist," in *Baptism and Eucharist: Ecumenical Convergence in Celebration* (Faith and Order Paper No. 117, ed. Max Thurian and Geoffrey Wainwright, Geneva: World Council of Churches, and Grand Rapids: Wm. B. Eerdmans 1983), p. 99.
6. See ibid., 111–15, where the earliest texts that contain the patterns to be followed in later liturgies are those of Justin Martyr (ca. 150 CE) and Hippolytus (ca. 215 CE).
7. Mary T. Douglas, *Purity and Danger: An Analysis of Concepts of Pollution and Taboo* (London: Routledge & Kegan Paul 1966), 61.
8. Ibid., 62.

2. The Greco-Roman Banquet: Defining a Common Meal Tradition

1. The origins and social meaning of the custom of reclining in the Greek world have been traced by means of a detailed study of Greek funerary monuments which use the motif of the deceased pictured reclining at a banquet. See Jean-Marie Dentzer, *Le motif du banquet couché dans le proche-orient et le monde grec du VIIIe au IVe siècle avant J.-C.* (Rome: École française de Rome 1982).
2. Oxyrhynchus papyri 2678 (3rd century CE) and 2791 (2nd century CE) respectively.
3. A recent translation of the Iobakchoi inscription is found in F. W. Danker, *Benefactor: Epigraphic Study of a Graeco-Roman and New Testament Semantic Field* (St Louis: Clayton Publishing House 1982), 156–66.
4. On Greek clubs, see especially Franz Poland, *Geschichte des griechischen Vereinswesens* (Leipzig: Teubner 1909).

5. A study of the symposium motif in Luke is found in Dennis E. Smith, "Table Fellowship as a Literary Motif in the Gospel of Luke," *Journal of Biblical Literature* 106 (1987), 613–38.

6. Mary Douglas, "Deciphering a Meal," *Daedalus* 101 (1972), 61.

7. Text and translation in Colin Roberts, T. C. Skeat and A. D. Nock, "The Guild of Zeus Hypsistos," *Harvard Theological Review* 29 (1936), 40–2.

8. An example: "Since the god invites all men to the feast and provides a table shared in common and offering equal privilege to those who come from whatever place they may come . . ." Inscription printed in *Bulletin de correspondance hellénique* 51 (1927), 73f.; translation by Dennis E. Smith.

3. The New Testament Banquet: Improvising on a Common Theme

1. An example is the classic work by Hans Lietzmann, *Mass and Lord's Supper* (Leiden: E. J. Brill, 1953–55).

2. Matthew's version of the eucharistic sayings (Matthew 26:26–29) is a virtual copy of Mark's with only a few editorial revisions. However, it should be noted that the cumulative effect of those revisions is to produce still another variation in the overall interpretation of the eucharistic sayings traditions. See further on Matthew below.

3. See a summary discussion of these issues in Eduard Schweizer, *The Lord's Supper According to the New Testament* (Facet Books 18; Philadelphia: Fortress Press 1967) 10–17.

4. Here the classic study is Joachim Jeremias, *The Eucharistic Words of Jesus* (London: SCM Press [3]1966), who argues that the last meal of Jesus was a passover meal and that the eucharistic sayings represent Jesus' own application of passover theology to an interpretation of his death.

5. On this point see also John Reumann, *The Supper of the Lord* (Philadelphia: Fortress Press 1985), 2–6.

6. On this point see Burton L. Mack, *A Myth of Innocence: Mark and Christian Origins* (Philadelphia: Fortress Press 1988), 116–20.

7. See the discussion of this text in Chapter 2 above, page 27.

8. Norman Perrin, *Rediscovering the Teaching of Jesus* (London: SCM Press and New York: Harper & Row 1967) 102–8.

9. See Mack, *A Myth of Innocence*, 188.

10. For a recent profile of the Jesus movement as sketched out here, see ibid., 78–97.

11. The existence of layers of tradition in Q has been established by John S. Kloppenborg, *The Formation of Q: Trajectories in Ancient Wisdom Collections* (Studies in Antiquity and Christianity, Philadelphia: Fortress Press 1987). A recent study by Burton L. Mack has proposed a social context for these developments; see "The Kingdom That Didn't Come: A Social History of the Q Tradents," *Society of Biblical Literature 1988 Seminar Papers* (ed. David J. Lull, Atlanta: Scholars Press 1988), 608–35.

12. These arguments are derived from Robert M. Fowler, *Loaves and Fishes: The Function of the Feeding Stories in the Gospel of Mark* (SBL Dissertation Series 54, Chico, CA: Scholars Press 1981), 132–8. For further studies that point out the literary nature of Mark's passion narrative, see

Werner H. Kelber (ed.), *The Passion in Mark: Studies on Mark 14–16* (Philadelphia: Fortress Press 1976), especially the essay by Vernon K. Robbins, "Last Meal: Preparation, Betrayal, and Absence," 21–40.

13. Fowler, *Loaves and Fishes*, 132–8.

14. This standard outline of Mark 8–10 is derived from Norman Perrin and Dennis C. Duling, *The New Testament: An Introduction* (New York: Harcourt Brace Jovanovich [2]1982), 248–51.

15. On martyrdom as the model for the death of Jesus in Mark, see Mack, *A Myth of Innocence*, 261–8.

16. See further Dennis E. Smith, "Table Fellowship as a Literary Motif in the Gospel of Luke," *Journal of Biblical Literature* 106 (1987), 613–38.

17. See ibid., 628 n. 44, for further discussion of this point.

18. On this point, see especially Robert H. Gundry, *Matthew: A Commentary on His Literary and Theological Art* (Grand Rapids: William B. Eerdmans 1982), 527f.

19. This interpretation is followed by many scholars. It receives its strongest statement in Rudolf Bultmann, *The Gospel of John: A Commentary* (Oxford: Blackwell and Philadelphia: The Westminster Press 1971), 218–37.

20. On this point, see especially Jacob Neusner, *The Ideal of Purity in Ancient Judaism* (Studies in Judaism in Late Antiquity, Leiden: E. J. Brill 1973), and Alan F. Segal, "Romans 7 and Jewish Dietary Laws," in *The Other Judaisms of Late Antiquity* (Brown Judaic Studies 127, Atlanta: Scholars Press 1987), 167–94.

21. See, e.g., this text from *Mishnah Abodah Zarah* 2:3: "These things belonging to Gentiles are prohibited . . . wine, vinegar of Gentiles which to begin with was wine . . . Meat which is being brought into an idol is permitted. But that which comes out is prohibited . . ." See the discussion of this text in Segal, "Romans 7 and Jewish Dietary Laws," 176f.

22. On this interpretation see especially Günther Bornkamm, "Lord's Supper and Church in Paul," *Early Christian Experience* (London: SCM Press and New York: Harper & Row 1969), 123–60, esp. 143–9.

23. This point has been especially argued by Gerd Theissen, "Social Integration and Sacramental Activity: An Analysis of 1 Cor. 11:17–34," in *The Social Setting of Pauline Christianity: Essays on Corinth*, ed. John H. Schuetz (Philadelphia: Fortress Press 1982), 145–74.

24. Helmut Koester, *Introduction to the New Testament. Volume 2: History and Literature of Early Christianity* (New York & Berlin: Walter De Gruyter 1982), 158–9.

25. It should be noted that the order of cup benediction followed by bread benediction would also represent a normal variation in customary meal practices. While in some contexts wine was apparently drunk only during the symposium course, in other contexts it was drunk during the meal. Here in Luke, then, as in the Jewish passover liturgy in the Mishnah, the meal begins with a benediction over the first cup of wine.

4. Celebrating at Many Tables Today

1. For instance, in Luke 10:38–42 Martha is a "deacon" (see Greek) who serves at table. Compare this to Acts 6:1–6.

2. The Lord's Day is mentioned explicitly in the Revelation to John 1:10, and the Gospel of John identifies the first day of the week with the resurrection (20:1) and with weekly gatherings of the disciples after the resurrection (20:19, 26). These references probably should not be taken as historical, but as indications of an attachment of the Johannine community to the Lord's day (first day of the week) as a time for gathering. Acts 2:26 and 5:42 are the Lukan evidence of daily gathering, although there are serious questions about this as an indicator of either Lukan or post-resurrection practice. Paul refers to gatherings for the Lord's Supper, although this does not seem to be necessarily on a weekly basis throughout his field of influence. The Jesus tradition points to gatherings at meals (e.g. Matthew 11:18, 19; Mark 2:15–17; Luke 14:15–24), but these gatherings seemed to be occasioned by invitations and other social occasions, rather than a regular rhythm.

3. The following examples are named fictitiously, but represent actual church situations.

5. Eucharistic Theory: Imaging Eternal Truth or Nurturing Social Reality?

1. Arnold van Gennep, *The Rites of Passage* (Chicago: The University of Chicago Press 1969, published originally in French in 1909).

2. Gerhard van der Leeuw, *Religion in Essence and Manifestation: A Study in Phenomology* (New York: Harper & Row 1963). This was originally published under the German title *Phänomenologie der Religion* in 1933.

3. Developed by Rudolf Otto in his book *The Idea of the Holy* (London: Oxford University Press 1929). Eliade recognizes his debt to Otto and makes a distinction between his work and Otto's in *The Sacred and the Profane* (New York: Harcourt, Brace and World 1968) pp. 8–10.

4. Mircea Eliade, *The Sacred and the Profane*.

5. Eliade, *The Sacred and the Profane*, 33.

6. Eliade, *The Sacred and the Profane*, 6.

7. Perhaps Eliade's most classic example is that of the Achilpa tribe of the Arunta people in Australia. These nomadic people set up sacred poles as they wander. Eliade proposes that it is the setting of the sacred pole that allows these people to see their particular setting as non-chaotic and organizable. He goes on to suggest that this is the same function of many rituals occurring in Western cathedrals and throughout the world (*The Sacred and the Profane*, 35–68).

8. Eliade, *The Sacred and the Profane*, 20ff.

9. Eliade, *The Sacred and the Profane*, 51.

10. Carl G. Jung, *Man and His Symbols* (New York: Dell 1964), 64.

11. *Collected Works of C. G. Jung*, Volume 9.

12. Van der Leeuw, *Religion in Essence and Manifestation*, II, 362.

13. For Lévi-Strauss's main proposals see his *Structural Anthropology* (New York, 1963).

14. See Turner's essay, "White Symbols in Literature and Religion," published in *Revelation and Divination in Ndembu Ritual* (Ithaca, NY: Cornell University Press 1975). Here Turner compares the meaning of white symbols in as diverse contexts as Ndembu ritual, New Testament texts, and Hermann Melville's *Moby Dick*, and proposes that they all signify the "act of being."

15. Turner, *Revelation and Divination in Ndembu Ritual*, 23.

16. In his essay on "Sacred Persistence" and his first chapter of *To Take Place: Toward Theory in Ritual*. Particularly devastating is Smith's treatment of Eliade's standard example of sacred space in the Achilpa ritual. Smith reviews carefully the data Eliade used to make his conclusions about the rationale for the nomadic Achilpa ritually planting the poles as they wander. Smith finds that in the dozens of accounts about the ritual stationing of a pole or other object during the wanderings of the Achilpa there is only one reference to the pole in relationship to any kind of cosmic orientation. Furthermore, he finds that almost every reference to such poles has a story about the appearance of an ancestor. In other words, Smith says, the ritual planting of the poles by the Achilpa has nothing to do with a kind of cosmic centering for a nomadic folk. Rather, it seems to be a way that the Achilpa, who in contrast to those of us who have stable homes do not orient themselves through fixed spatial realities, have of keeping in contact with the memory (presence?) of their ancestors. Smith shows that Eliade has ignored most of the anthropological data in order to highlight one small portion of a non-Western ritual that he can parallel with Western notions of the sacred.

17. J. Z. Smith, *To Take Place: Toward Theory in Ritual*.

18. J. Z. Smith, *Imagining Religion* (Chicago: University of Chicago Press 1982), 100f.

19. J. M. Kitagawa, "Ainu Bear Festival (Iyomante)," *History of Religions* I (1961), 95–151; M. Eliade, *Shamanism*, 158–164.

20. A. I. Hallowell, "Bear Ceremonialism in the Northern Hemisphere," *American Anthropologist* 28 (1926), 1–175.

21. A recent and strong case for this was made by Walter Burkert in *Homo Necans*, 1–93, in which he parallels such prehistoric ceremonial killing with Greek drama. Burkhert has also paralleled this prehistoric killing with the Christian eucharistic sacrifice, a parallel strongly challenged by Smith. For the discussion between these two scholars on ritual killing and sacrifice, see Robert Hammerton-Kelly, ed., *Violent Origins* (Stanford: Stanford University Press 1986).

22. J. Z. Smith, "The Bare Facts of Ritual," *Imagining Religion*, 63.

23. J. Z. Smith, *To Take Place: Toward Theory in Ritual*.

24. Mary Douglas, *Purity and Danger: An Analysis of the Concepts of Pollution and Taboo* (London: Routledge and Kegan Paul 1966).

25. "Deciphering a Meal," 61–81.

26. *Revelation and Divination in Ndembu Ritual*, 23.

27. There is, of course, a major problem with this theological approach. If God is primarily encountered in the *communitas*, then what is God's relationship to the non-human spheres? The direction of Turner's suggestion does conveniently link ritual's function of nourishing social reality with Christian theology of God in the community of the faithful, but perhaps only by also maintaining a long-standing Christian bias against the non-human. A God encountered primarily in the community of the faithful seems to be a God who is only secondarily, if at all, present in trees, winds, oceans, and galaxies. Such a human-centered theology is not helpful, for example, in addressing ecological issues. One possible theological integration of Turner's "theology of ritual" would be an implicitly polytheistic one. One could see "Christ" as the "God of the community," while reserving more expansive realms for other partners in the trinity or other gods.

6. Eucharistic Liturgies for Different Social Settings Today

1. Matthew Fox, *The Coming of the Cosmic Christ* (San Francisco: Harper & Row 1988).
2. Susan Cady, *Wisdom's Feast: Sophia in Study and Celebration*, (San Francisco: Harper & Row 1989), 102.
3. See Susan Cady, Marian Ronan and Hal Taussig, *Wisdom's Feast*, for additional information and eucharistic liturgies on Wisdom.

Index to Ancient Sources

Greek Authors